"Papa Don is the Caleb of the end times, a man of faith in a great God. Our Messiah Jesus encourages you to be bold as a lion, to overcome by the blood of the Lamb and the word of your testimony, and not to love your life to the death. *The Handbook for the End Times* is a must-read for such a time as this!"

Samaa Habib, author, *Face to Face with Jesus*

"Many teach on what could happen in the end times, but what has been glaringly lacking is sound teaching on how to live in the end times. It is extremely helpful to know how to read the signs of the times, but then what? Then comes the trustworthy voice of Don Finto instructing us how to respond and not overreact, how to walk in faith and not in fear and how to be prepared! Be not taken off guard; rather, be salt and light. Be prepared for such a time as this."

James W. Goll, founder, God Encounters Ministries;
trainer, Life Language Communications;
international speaker and author

"I wish that every young leader would heed the wisdom and zeal that Don Finto pours out on the pages of this book. In a time with so much confusion, this book comes as a clarion call on how we ought to live now and in the days ahead! Young leaders, let us soak up the words of this time-tested spiritual father and truly live faith-filled lives!"

Andy Byrd, School of the Circuit Rider; Fire and Fragrance
Ministries; University of the Nations, Kona, Hawaii

"Don Finto has a declaration for the Christian Church today: Be prepared for more dark times ahead. I am encouraged, though, because this wise man, with the prompting of Holy Spirit, has given us *The Handbook for the End Times*. We will survive and even thrive in these last days, and we are called to be the light of Jesus in every time."

Heidi Baker, co-founder and CEO, Iris Global

THE
HANDBOOK
FOR THE
**END
TIMES**

THE
HANDBOOK
FOR THE

END
TIMES

Hope, Help and Encouragement

FOR LIVING IN THE LAST DAYS

DON FINTO

Chosen

a division of Baker Publishing Group
Minneapolis, Minnesota

Published by Chosen Books
11400 Hampshire Avenue South
Bloomington, Minnesota 55438
www.chosenbooks.com

Chosen Books is a division of
Baker Publishing Group, Grand Rapids, Michigan

Printed in the United States of America

ISBN 978-0-8007-9899-4

Library of Congress Control Number: 2017963662

18   19   20   21   22   23   24   7   6   5   4   3   2   1

Dedicated to the memory of a godly woman
Martha Graves Finto
my wife and closest friend for 64 years
a devoted mother, grandmother and friend,
and an ardent follower of Jesus through life
November 3, 1929—March 10, 2016

Contents

Foreword

It was Don Finto's wonderful book *Your People Shall Be My People* that first awakened me to the two great biblical signposts heralding the global entrance into the last days. I felt as if I were listening to the old man Daniel, that biblical prophet, who unfolded the last days understanding that was gained through extended fasting and prayer. I felt I was being tutored by a great man of the Scriptures—a man who had walked a journey of integrity, passion, power and prophecy. The nation of Israel and the Jewish people had not yet captured my heart. But my eyes lit up when I understood in depth the place Israel has in the last days scenario.

Right in the pages of Don's book, I found my name being called and found my place in the story. I realized I was not just to be fasting and interceding for the Gentile nations. I was to be a Daniel, interceding for the nation of Israel and calling others into that intercession as well.

For years now, inspired by Joel 2, I have been calling massive, solemn assemblies of fasting and prayer for the outpouring of the Spirit and the shifting of nations.

The real story of Joel 2, however, is not just the fast, but the *outcome* of the fast. Joel unveils two major signposts: After the fast, God promises to (1) restore the land of Israel and (2) pour out His Holy Spirit on the Gentiles.

In 1948 a worldwide fasting movement was initiated through a book called *Atomic Power with God through Fasting and Prayer*. Then came the outpouring called (from Joel 2) the "Latter Rain." In that same year, Jewish people were returning to their land and the nation of Israel was established through the vote of the United Nations—or, should I say, through the hand of the Lord.

In 1967, with the utopian dream of the 1960s spiraling into a nightmare of war, assassinations, riots and disillusionment, another Joel 2 cry ascended into heaven. Again God answered with the two signs. First, Jerusalem was recaptured by the Jewish military in the Six-Day War and became the capital of Israel, the sign of the restoration of the land. Second, outpourings of the Holy Spirit took place around the globe through the Jesus People movement and charismatic renewal. Then Jewish believers began returning to Messiah in great numbers, inaugurating the beginning of the last days rollout described in Romans 11:12–15.

When Daniel understood it was time for the restoration of Jerusalem and the rebuilding of the Temple, he set his face to fasting and prayer. It has been seven decades since Israel's rebirth as a nation in 1948. More and more Jewish people are coming to their Messiah than ever before. We can feel the birth pangs of the new day and the unfolding of last days prophecy.

Don Finto's newest book, *The Handbook for the End Times*, is leading us into another stage of understanding and revelation for what is soon to take place. Once again I sense that I am under the tutelage of a Daniel. I can feel, through a prophetic father, the heart of God, who wants not only to point out the signs of the times but to prepare His children to go through the fires, storms and persecutions that Scripture foretells. This is not a book that causes us to stick our heads in the sand and ignore the dark side of biblical prophecy. It confronts us with the need to be aware of the persecution, deception and world upheaval ahead. Yet it does not focus on the negative. Instead it is poised to inject faith into the Body of Christ for greater victories to come. For although darkness covers the earth, the glory of the Lord will shine upon you.

The last days will be the greatest days of the Church. All hell will not quench her fire, her passion and her victory. Testimonies of Christ's dominion, similar to those in the book of Daniel, will be demonstrated even while powers of darkness rage. Clearly the letters in the book of Revelation that were sent to the angels of the churches will be manifested. The voice of the Lord will declare: "He who overcomes . . . TO HIM I WILL GIVE AUTHORITY OVER THE NATIONS" (Revelation 2:26 NASB). This motivates me!

I have not experienced the pain of persecution as in the Middle East, North Korea, Northern Africa and other places. Even so, I can hardly focus on the dark side because of the brightness of the rising King. Every tribe and tongue will receive a witness of the Gospel. Principalities and powers will be driven from their heavenly lairs that have lain undisturbed for centuries. With Don Finto, I refuse the counsel of despair and a jaded vision of the future. The Lord reigns; let the earth tremble before Him!

Don lifts up the Bible hero Caleb, who saw the Promised Land and was willing to face giants rather than wander for forty years in the wilderness. Like Don, I have seen, by dreams, the prophetic Promised Land. I will not live my life under the shadow of statistics, failure and doom-and-gloom prognosticators. I am living under the shadow of the dominating prophecy that this book heralds.

The Handbook for the End Times is filled with hope, and it gives us pastoral and prophetic instruction—not just on how to survive, but on how to flourish with wisdom and understanding in the middle of coming upheaval and deception. We would all do well to sit under this Daniel and his instruction, to heed the warnings, to be encouraged by the amazing stories and to glean from the skilled exegesis of Scripture and descriptions of history.

Brothers and sisters, Jesus is coming again, and this book is preparing us for that coming. It will be, first of all, a coming of His presence, releasing testimonies of Kingdom reformation in the midst of horrific opposition. It will be a coming with historic waves of revival and spiritual awakening. And then it will be the Second Coming with the sound of the trumpet, when He will put His feet on the earth, crushing kings in the day of battle and establishing His full dominion from sea to sea. He will set up His throne and secure peace for the nations. Oh, yes, the devil will do his best to wage war and to rage against the people of God, but Jesus Christ Himself shall conquer the beast and reign.

So take hold of this book and read. Then run with mighty faith into the future, knowing you have been given a role to play on the last days stage of history.

Lou Engle, co-founder, TheCall; founder, Bound 4 Life

Acknowledgments

Scripture calls us to "enter His gates with thanksgiving" (Psalm 100:4) and to bring our prayers and petitions to God "with thanksgiving" (Philippians 4:6; Colossians 4:2). I am a very blessed man. I am forgiven, I am counted as righteous and I have an inheritance that is eternal. I was blessed with a faithful wife of 64 years, have a family who loves me and loves each other and have an extended family that reaches around the world.

Our Caleb family—I smile every time I am among or even think about them—are scattered among the nations. They are an intergenerational group of passionate, godly, prayerful, worshiping, hungry disciples of Jesus. They challenge, inspire and encourage me.

What can I say to the Lord for having brought Tod McDowell and me together? In the spring of 2005, while I was teaching in the Kona, Hawaii, Youth With A Mission base, God prophetically/supernaturally brought Tod into my life as a spiritual son. He was already a general in the Lord's army, destined to lead His people forward into strength and power as we move hastily toward Jesus' return. He has expressed himself personally in the chapter on the Holy Spirit.

Tod is now director of the Caleb Company, a ministry I started in late 1996 with the desire to raise up an army like the biblical Caleb who would (1) take their mountains when they are 85 and beyond, (2) stay wholeheartedly devoted to the Lord all their days and (3) raise up the generations behind them. Our desire is to equip the Church to understand, embrace and participate in God's biblical plan for Israel and the Jewish people, and its relationship to world awakening and revival in our day.

I would be arrogantly remiss if I pretended to have written without the aid of Anne Severance. She is a gentle, humble and gifted woman of God who has taught and continues to teach me how to put into words what my heart is trying to say. Thank you, Anne, for being there for *Your People Shall Be My People*, for *God's Promise and the Future of Israel* and now for *The Handbook for the End Times*.

Thank you, Jane Campbell and Baker Publishing Group, for entrusting to me the honor of being a Chosen author and for helping to "produce weapons of mass instruction," as we were prophetically told to do. May this book be indeed one of those weapons that will challenge the Church to stand strong even in times of great distress.

Introduction

Strange how Scripture that we have read dozens, even hundreds of times, will suddenly take on fresh revelation. This happened to me a few years ago when I was reading Jesus' parable of the wheat and weeds, as recorded in the thirteenth chapter of Matthew. I was struck by the fact that Jesus was describing the end of our age, when both world righteousness and world wickedness reach their maturity simultaneously and are ready to be harvested.

Jesus' description of the end times makes me believe that those famous opening phrases from Dickens's *The Tale of Two Cities* were never more appropriate than in the days just ahead of us: "It was the best of times, it was the worst of times, it was the age of wisdom, it was the age of foolishness, it was the epoch of belief, it was the epoch of incredulity, it was the season of Light, it was the season of Darkness."

The darkest time in all of history, as well as the most brilliant for the people of God, lies before us. It is the exciting possibilities of this next season that compelled me to write this book.

While the quotation by Charles Dickens comes from a classic English novel of the nineteenth century, Jesus' parable of the wheat and weeds is Jesus' own description of the days ahead.

Several years ago I became captivated by Jesus' words in Luke 21 concerning the destruction of Jerusalem, the scattering of the Jewish people among the nations and the Gentile domination of that city for a season until the time came for the Jewish people to regain control of their capital. The revelation that began coming to me inspired me to write *Your People Shall Be My People* and *God's Promise and the Future of Israel*. The thesis of both books has to do with the timing of God in our generation, a time in which Jewish people by the tens of thousands are beginning to believe that Yeshua/Jesus is indeed the promised Messiah and the corresponding awakening of faith among the nations that Jesus is not only Israel's Messiah but the world Redeemer—all this at a time when evil in the world is also rapidly accelerating.

My own personal awakening led me to take a harder look at Israel's prophets, as well as the end time messages of Jesus and the apostles.

Many believe that Spirit-empowered believers will be "taken away" before our enemy launches his last great assault. I see many reasons for rejecting that theory and for the need to expend our energy preparing to weather the coming storms and shine most brilliantly during the world's darkest hour.

I am learning to trust the Word of God even when I do not understand it. Another verse I have quoted for years and believe *most* of the time is Romans 8:28. I have read these words in various versions just to be sure I am not misreading Paul's core thought.

And we know that in all things God works for the good of those who love him, who have been called according to his purpose (NIV).

We know [with great confidence] that God [who is deeply concerned about us] causes all things to work together [as a plan] for good to those who love God, to those who are called according to His plan and purpose (AMP).

And we know that God causes all things to work together for good for those who love God, to those who are called according to His purpose (NASB).

All things!
All!
For good!

Not for everyone but for those who love the Lord and are called by Him.

One of my close friends once preached a sermon entitled "The Most Difficult Verse in the Bible to Believe." It was Romans 8:28! I happened to be in the congregation that day and was surprised at the verse he had chosen. Yet I found myself immediately agreeing with him.

Even though I have quoted the verse almost my entire life, I still find it impossible to grasp—except that I know God is always right. No matter how grim the situation, how intense the suffering, no matter how evil the consequences, He finds a way to mold all the circumstances for good for those of us who have embraced Him as our Leader.

In looking back over my own life, I see how true Paul's words are. I would never have chosen for my own father to abandon the family, for my mother to die or for me to experience sexual molestation from a trusted preacher cousin as a way of drawing me into the heart of God. But I realize that God used the confusion of that time and godly grandparents to compel me to know Him even at an early age.

How could I have known that God would use that childhood trauma to make me more desperate for Him and more willing to follow Him? But God knew the call He wanted to place on my life and was using every circumstance to mold me into that destiny. My role was to keep loving Him and trusting Him.

Now, a few years later and after a lifetime of learning to believe this verse, I am about to tell you of some things that are predicted in Scripture that do not sound good at all. Still, I believe completely that God will work all the bad stuff that is coming in the future for our good if we will simply hang onto Him and trust Him.

Jesus' words have motivated me to challenge the people of God to become the most radical, God-empowered and God-empowering, miracle-working, people-rescuing followers of Jesus in the history of the planet. So join me on the pilgrimage. Do not be afraid when you read about or even experience some of the horrors that will come. The best is yet ahead! Keep remembering Romans 8:28. And in case you should be tempted to forget along the way, I will keep reminding you.

1

Let Both Grow Together

"Take your sickle and reap, because the time to reap has
come, for the harvest of the earth is ripe."

Revelation 14:15

Seven words out of Jesus' end time parable of the wheat and
the weeds have changed the way I look at the future: *Let both
grow together until the harvest.*

Jesus was telling one of those the-Kingdom-of-heaven-is-like
parables. A man sowed good seed in his field, but an enemy
came and sowed weeds. As the plants began to grow, the field
hands seem to have seen nothing unusual. Only as the plants
"sprouted and formed heads" did they detect the weeds (see
Matthew 13:26–39).

The servants asked the master, "Do you want us to go and
pull them up?"

"No," he answered, "because while you are pulling the weeds,
you may uproot the wheat with them. *Let both grow together
until the harvest.* At that time I will tell the harvesters: First
collect the weeds and tie them in bundles to be burned, then
gather the wheat and bring it into my barn."

The disciples may have been thinking, *Good story! But we still do not understand what He is saying.*

"Explain to us the parable of the weeds in the field," they later asked Jesus.

So He went into greater detail, detail that gives very clear meaning to those seven words.

> "The one who sowed the good seed is the Son of Man. The field is the world, and the good seed stands for the people of the kingdom. The weeds are the people of the evil one, and the enemy who sows them is the devil. The harvest is the end of the age, and the harvesters are angels."
>
> Matthew 13:37–39

I have read these words dozens of times, but not until a few years ago did I get the basic message Jesus was communicating to His friends, as well as to us these many centuries later. This is the end time of all end time parables. Jesus is describing what is to happen at the close of the age—this age, the age in which we now live. At the time of God's choosing, there will be a harvest of both wickedness and righteousness, of both the wicked and the righteous.

Premature Harvest

I am a West Texas farm boy. I know what it means to harvest when something is ripe. We were cotton farmers. Try to harvest cotton too early and it is worthless. Not even when that white begins to show inside the boll would one dare to pick the cotton. Still worthless! One must be patient. But when the boll is fully open, grab the cotton quickly, take it to the market and sell it for enough money to feed the family for the year.

There is an interesting little aside in the encounter Abraham had with God when He was describing what would happen to

Abraham's descendants: "For four hundred years your descendants will be strangers in a country not their own and . . . they will be enslaved and mistreated" (Genesis 15:13). And then He gave one of the reasons for Israel's long estrangement from their country of destiny. "In the fourth generation your descendants will come back here, *for the sin of the Amorites has not yet reached its full measure*" (verse 16, emphasis added). Or, as the King James Version reads: "The iniquity of the Amorites is not yet full."

According to His communication with Abraham, God, in His sense of justice, cannot judge a nation—or, in the case of the wheat/weeds parable, the world—until the iniquity of that nation is full, has reached its full measure, has ripened.

Jesus' simple parable describes for us the time of the end for our present age, when world wickedness will reach its zenith, or, in this case, its nadir. When the sin tank of the world is full, God will bring down the curtain on world civilization in its present form.

These Are the Days

That is the bad news. But the good news is that while wickedness is ripening, righteousness is also ripening. Followers of Jesus will become the godliest, the most Holy Spirit–empowered, the purest of heart, the most miracle-working generation in the history of the planet. Jesus ended the explanation of the parable with words that attest to this maturing: "Then the righteous will shine like the sun in the kingdom of their Father" (Matthew 13:43).

Hundreds of years prior to Jesus' coming, the prophet Daniel saw the very thing Jesus described. He saw "the time of the end" (Daniel 12:4, 9) at "the end of the days" (verse 13), a time when "those who are wise will shine like the brightness of the heavens, and those who lead many to righteousness, like the stars for ever and ever" (verse 3). This will be a time when "many will be purified, made spotless and refined, but the wicked will continue to be wicked" (verse 10).

Interestingly enough, without any way to imagine airplane travel and superhighways in the nations of the world and without the remotest comprehension of an atomic age when the world's wisest scientists and scholars would be unable to keep up with all of the latest technologies and inventions, Daniel described the very era in which we are living, a time when "many will go back and forth, and knowledge will increase" (Daniel 12:4 NASB). Nothing in all of Scripture more precisely distinguishes our generation from all those in prior years. We indeed are going back and forth, with millions of us in the air, traveling from nation to nation at any given moment. Other multiple millions are traveling at high speeds on the world's highways.

At the same time knowledge is increasing at such astonishing speed that even those in the field of technology have trouble staying abreast—to say nothing of the fact that I can hold in my hand access to more knowledge than was in the world's finest libraries less than a century ago.

All this is happening at the same time that the wise, those who are leading many to righteousness, are growing into their destinies of "shining like the brightness of the heavens . . . like the stars," as Daniel foresaw.

Radical and Radiant

Remember when Moses came down from the mountain after being with God, and "the Israelites could not look steadily at the face of Moses because of its glory" (2 Corinthians 3:7)?

Have you ever pondered what it will be like when, as the psalmist predicts, "those who look to [God] are radiant" (Psalm 34:5)?

I love the story that was highlighted on *The 700 Club* some years back. A well-known Hollywood figure, a Jewish atheist known for his sometimes ruthless business practices, came upon extremely hard times. During this downturn in his professional life, his wife, too, could no longer tolerate his behavior and left with their child.

One night, in complete despair, this man walked out on the beach in front of his Malibu home, raised his hands to the God he did not believe in and cried, "Help!"

When he went back inside, Jesus appeared to him. The man was so undone by the encounter that he started calling some close friends to tell them what had happened. But they did not take the matter seriously, supposing that he had had too much alcohol or was high on some drug.

Weeks later, while at a Hollywood party, he was strangely drawn to a couple across the room. They seemed so at peace with themselves and with life. The way they greeted people, the manner in which they treated each other. Even their faces had almost a glow about them.

Though he had no idea who the couple was, he finally summoned the courage to walk up to them and inquire. "You're different, different from anyone else in this room," he said. "There is something about the way you relate to each other and to others here. What is this with you?"

They knew all about their inquirer. They knew of his amazing success in the movie industry, but they also knew that he could be ruthless and uncaring in order to get his way.

"Are you sure you want to know?" they answered cautiously.

"Yes, tell me."

"We are radical followers of Jesus," they said. "We believe that He is your Messiah, the promised One from the prophets. We believe He rose from the dead, and that He has sent His Spirit to live within us. We have come to know a peace that we had never before experienced. Maybe you would like to get to know Him as well."

And so it was that this former Jewish atheist, after telling them the story of his beachside cry and his late-night encounter, came to know his Messiah—all because of the countenance of two of Jesus' followers. The radiance of which the psalmist spoke, the radiance that shone in Moses' face, the brightness Daniel foresaw was playing out in the hearts and lives of a Hollywood couple, whom God used to bring another of His children into the Kingdom.

Harvest of Wrath and Righteousness

We are living the partial fulfillment of the promise, but we have yet to experience its fullness, its ripeness. Yet if Jesus' wheat-weeds parable is true—and we know that it is—then the time will come when the righteousness, the holiness, the purity, the empowering of believers will have reached its zenith among every tribe, tongue, nation and people—all who will stand before the throne of God in the last day (see Revelation 5:9; 7:9).

In the closing years of his life, the apostle John also saw and described the final harvest of which Jesus had spoken.

> I looked, and there before me was a white cloud, and seated on the cloud was one like a son of man with a crown of gold on his head and a sharp sickle in his hand. Then another angel came out of the temple and called in a loud voice to him who was sitting on the cloud, "Take your sickle and reap, because the time to reap has come, for the harvest of the earth is ripe." So he who was seated on the cloud swung his sickle over the earth, and the earth was harvested.
>
> Revelation 14:14–16

John saw the harvest of righteousness, but then he saw two additional angels who were involved in the harvest of the wicked.

Another angel came out of the temple in heaven, and he too had a sharp sickle. Still another angel, who had charge of the fire, came from the altar and called in a loud voice to him who had the sharp sickle, "Take your sharp sickle and gather the clusters of grapes from the earth's vine, because its grapes are ripe." The angel swung his sickle on the earth, gathered its grapes and threw them into the great winepress of God's wrath.

Revelation 14:17–19

One day near the close of Jesus' life, as He and His disciples were walking away from the Temple to the Mount of Olives, He brought up again the subject of the time of the end, as well as the destruction of the Temple that would occur when Rome destroyed the city in AD 70. There would be great upheavals, an "increase of wickedness, [when] the love of most will grow cold . . . [a time of] great distress, unequaled from the beginning of the world until now—and never to be equaled again" (Matthew 24:12, 21; see also Daniel 12:1). That is wickedness ripening.

But this will also be a time when "this gospel of the kingdom will be preached in the whole world as a testimony to all nations" (Matthew 24:14).

The "people of the evil one" will flourish, mature and ripen into the wickedest, the most lustful, the most terrorizing, the most idolatrous, the most selfish generation in the history of the world.

But at the same time, the "people of the Kingdom" will mature, flourish and ripen as we move into our destiny of becoming the most powerful, godly, miracle-working, radiant body of believers the world has ever known.

Both growing side by side until the end!

With what kind of attitude should we approach the ripening? What should we expect as the harvest nears? Come with me as we look at ways that will help us be a strong, vibrant part of the future, even when the times are difficult and dangerous.

2

Listen to the Right Report

Then Caleb silenced the people before Moses and said,
"We should go up and take possession of the land, for
we can certainly do it."

Numbers 13:30

Recently in Nashville word spread through the Christian
community that two strategic films were being previewed
at one of our local theaters. The films were to give helpful,
behind-the-scenes depictions of world events. I made plans
to attend.

On the night of the showing, the small theater was packed
to capacity with representatives from the believing community,
many of them friends of mine from a variety of congregations
across the city. An air of anticipation filled the room as we
settled in for the evening.

Not long into the showing of the first film, I began to feel
a certain discomfort. Everything being communicated seemed

to be true, but the "God factor" was missing. The film was a well-documented account of enemy activity and of plans for world domination, including the frightening inroads currently being made into our own nation.

Earlier in the day I had been reading of the unprecedented godly underground awakening in the very nations that were being described in the film. Yet nothing of those revivals was being reported.

By the time the first film concluded and the host came to the podium to introduce the second film, my uneasiness had increased. I do not recall his exact words, but I know what he seemed to be saying: "More than fifty years ago, Nazism threatened the entire world, but we defeated it. Then the dread of Communism was upon us, but that, too, has fallen. Now we are faced with an even more insidious enemy. Radical Islam is encroaching on our communities, our schools and our government. If this evil is not defeated, our country will become engulfed in a sea of mass terrorism."

As the second film began I made my way discreetly to the exit. I had been listening to the report of the ten spies. Why was there no mention of the "God factor," the great advances for the Gospel that are being made in the midst of darkness? Where were the voices of Caleb and Joshua? In retrospect, I should have been one of those voices. I could have encouraged people to stay strong, no matter what the future holds.

Not long after this experience I learned that another film was advertised for the same theater. Because of my acquaintance with those sponsoring the showing, I was present. The depiction was an end time movie in which believers were being persecuted—even to death—but the story was saturated with what I call "but-God" stories. Even though I left the theater that night knowing that we could be entering a time of great persecution, I was encouraged. The strength and faith of believers was evident in the lives of those depicted.

31

The Caleb and Joshua Vision

Every Sunday school student knows the story.

The journey from Horeb, the area around Sinai, to Kadesh Barnea in the southern desert of Israel was an eleven-day trip (see Deuteronomy 1:2).

But that journey lasted forty years!

Why?

Because the nation listened to the reports of the ten spies, not to those of Caleb and Joshua.

Twelve men, among them Caleb and Joshua, were given the assignment of exploring the land promised to them by God and bringing back a report to Moses and the children of Israel.

> When Moses sent them to explore Canaan, he said, "Go up through the Negev and on into the hill country. See what the land is like and whether the people who live there are strong or weak, few or many. What kind of land do they live in? Is it good or bad? What kind of towns do they live in? Are they unwalled or fortified? How is the soil? Is it fertile or poor? Are there trees in it or not? Do your best to bring back some of the fruit of the land."
>
> Numbers 13:17–20

For forty days, the twelve men followed their instructions faithfully, observing the cities of the region and their inhabitants. At the end of that time the spies brought back pomegranates and figs, along with a huge cluster of grapes so heavy that it had to be carried by two men.

All twelve saw the same things, but their accounts to Moses and the leaders of Israel were significantly different. Only Caleb and Joshua figured the "God factor" into the equation. They remembered the promises and they believed God. The other ten spies described only what they saw with their natural eyes, even at times exaggerating the danger in order to sway the crowd.

"The people who live there are powerful, and the cities are fortified and very large," the ten reported. "We even saw descendants of Anak there. . . . People we saw there are of great size. We saw the Nephilim" (Numbers 13:28, 32–33).

True. Factually accurate.

"They are stronger than we are. . . . The land we explored devours those living in it. . . . We seemed like grasshoppers in our own eyes, and we looked the same to them" (Numbers 13:31–33).

Stretching truth to make the point.

"The cities are large, with walls up to the sky" (Deuteronomy 1:28).

I think not. Over the top!

Caleb and Joshua were of an opposite spirit (see Numbers 14:24). They saw the same thing but judged differently. "We should go up and take possession of the land, for we can certainly do it," they implored (Numbers 13:30).

> "The land we passed through and explored is exceedingly good. If the LORD is pleased with us, he will lead us into that land, a land flowing with milk and honey, and will give it to us. Only do not rebel against the LORD. And do not be afraid of the people of the land, because we will devour them. Their protection is gone, but the LORD is with us. Do not be afraid of them."
>
> Numbers 14:7–9

Days of the Giants

The Church is reliving the days of the giants. The circumstances around us are bewildering and foreboding. Two voices are dominant. One is the voice of fear that describes walled cities and giants. The other is the beckoning of God to a life of faith and victory over every enemy.

"What are we going to do?" asks the first voice. "We are in total moral decay. More than half of our marriages end in divorce. More and more of our young people are living together outside of marriage. Homosexuality is on the rise. Abortion statistics are staggering. Infanticide and euthanasia are on the horizon. Natural disasters are increasing. The price of oil is making normal living impossible. Bankruptcies are skyrocketing. Our leaders are no longer dependable. Our school systems are being infiltrated with textbooks that have rewritten history and advocate godless lifestyles. Our nation is out from under the protection of God. Even the Church is filled with greed, pride and immorality."

These are accurate descriptions, but if we draw our conclusions from these reports we will not hear the voice of the Holy Spirit.

Is the world economy in danger? Yes.

Is terrorism rampant? Yes.

Are natural disasters intensifying? Is greed controlling the world? Are people of God being persecuted, imprisoned and even executed for their faith? Yes. Yes. Yes.

But there is another side of the story.

In the midst of the deepening darkness, great light is appearing. Nations long held in bondage are hearing of the freedom that comes from the Jewish Messiah who has become Redeemer of all the nations. The greatest revival in history is upon us.

Fearless in Faith

My own nation, the United States, has often exhibited only a veneer of Christian faith. Such a faith will not be adequate for the future.

But there is a rising body of Holy Spirit–empowered believers in many other parts of the world that not only has accepted the first two phrases of John's vision regarding power over the enemy—"They triumphed over [Satan] by the blood of the Lamb and by the word of their testimony"—but also has embraced the third phrase: "They did not love their lives so much as to shrink from death" (Revelation 12:11).

A proverbial expression from the early centuries of faith states that "the blood of the martyrs is the seed of the Kingdom." No power of hell can defeat believers who are sold out to the Lord.

A recent report from a group of believers in the Middle East tells of thirteen people who were baptized to proclaim their allegiance to Jesus, their newly found Savior. Within two weeks, eleven of them were dead—"honor killings"—murdered by families who would not tolerate other members forsaking the family religion.

Yet this report is from one of the countries where faith in Jesus is advancing with amazing speed. Great persecution often brings in an even greater harvest of souls.

"Let Them Kill Me!"

I recall my only visit to China. The year was 1989, soon after the Beijing uprising that took the lives of hundreds if not thousands of young people in Tiananmen Square. Our group had traveled to Hong Kong, making repeated trips across the border into Guangzhou, always loaded with Bibles hidden in our luggage and praying to get through the checkpoint undetected. On one particular day we flew from Guangzhou to Beijing, with multiple suitcases filled with Bibles that were to be distributed to underground Church pastors. When we arrived after midnight in Beijing, the airport had closed, so we were able to grab our luggage and head to the hotel.

The following morning we set out to take the Bibles to the home of "Sister Mabel." She greeted us with great joy and ushered us into her tiny apartment. One whole wall was piled high with Bibles and study materials, waiting to be delivered to pastors who would be risking their lives to receive them.

"Aren't you afraid to keep all these Bibles so clearly visible in your apartment?" one of our group asked Sister Mabel.

"What can they do to me?" she answered with a shrug. "I've been in prison. Let them kill me. I'll only see Jesus more quickly."

Sister Mabel's work is still thriving though she has long since gone to be with the Lord. One of the young men who used to go to Sister Mabel's apartment to collect her Bibles and take them to pastors in the underground Church movement was the son of Peter Xu, who today leads a network of house churches numbering into the millions. Peter, Enoch Wang and Brother Yun, current Chinese leaders whom we have visited recently, have endured a total of almost forty years in prison for their faith.[1]

Faith Involves Risk

During the 1920s, long before the great upsurge of believers in their nation, the "Back to Jerusalem" vision was born in the hearts of a few of China's believers. They *saw* one hundred thousand missionaries taking the Gospel to the Buddhists of Southeast Asia, through the Hindu strongholds of northern India and then finally flourishing in the Muslim nations of central Asia, all the way to the Middle East and Israel. They knew that these men and women of God would be risking their lives to bring the Gospel, but they were listening to the Caleb/Joshua voice of the Holy Spirit rather than to the fears of man.

In 1995 Rolland and Heidi Baker[2] went to Mozambique, Africa. They had no contacts and no money, but they had a vision. Mozambique was one of the poorest nations on earth and had been ravaged by almost thirty years of civil war. In the last decades, the Bakers and their co-workers have poured out their lives for the poor, preached the Gospel of Jesus and cared for thousands of children, widows, single mothers and others in need. Like Paul, they have experienced shipwrecks, sleepless nights, hunger, life-threatening diseases, stones and curses being hurled at them and more, but they have also found those closing verses in Mark's gospel to be true: "The Lord worked with them and confirmed his word by the signs that accompanied it" (Mark 16:20). I have been to Pemba, Mozambique, and have personally witnessed the lame walking, the blind seeing and the deaf-mute speaking.

Iris Global Ministry is now active in fifteen nations with a network of churches that exceeds ten thousand. They operate five Bible schools for both African pastors and international students, in addition to their three primary schools and school of missions in Pemba.

During mid-2014 thousands of rockets were launched into Israel from Gaza, the very land Israel had forfeited in an attempt to make peace with their neighbors. Some of us visited Israel during those days and found strong believers who were not holed up in bunkers day and night but were using the opportunity to take food and supplies to those who were not able to leave their homes. They were light in the darkness and found people even more open to the Gospel of Jesus during the attacks.

A similar thing was happening in Northern Iraq. Believers were using their church buildings and their homes to house refugees. A small group of young Israelis left the greater comfort of their own homes in the Jerusalem area and made their way through Turkey into Northern Iraq in order to deliver aid to the suffering.

Believers who are listening to Holy Spirit, the Calebs and Joshuas of our generation, are not afraid of the future. We know the storms are coming, but we are walking with the One who controls the storms and who can keep us safe even when in danger.

Words Giving Life

The voices of the ten spies say, "Be careful! Protect yourself! Don't take chances!"

The voices of Caleb and Joshua say, "Don't be afraid. Put your trust in the Lord. Walk in His power, His strength. You were brought to the Kingdom for these days. Yield your life as a holy instrument that ministers in His strength." Scripture assures us:

> Even in darkness light dawns for the upright, for those who are gracious and compassionate and righteous.
>
> Psalm 112:4

> Darkness covers the earth and thick darkness is over the peoples, but the LORD rises upon you and his glory appears over you.
>
> Isaiah 60:2

> Under his wings you will find refuge; his faithfulness will be your shield and rampart. You will not fear the terror of night, nor the arrow that flies by day, nor the pestilence that stalks in the darkness, nor the plague that destroys at midday. A thousand may fall at your side, ten thousand at your right hand, but it will not come near you.
>
> Psalm 91:4–7

> Do not be anxious about anything, but in every situation, by prayer and petition, with thanksgiving, present your requests to God. And the peace of God, which transcends all understanding, will guard your hearts and your minds in Christ Jesus.
>
> Philippians 4:6–7

Paul cried out that last admonition to the Philippians from a Roman jail. These are not simply nice declarations for church liturgy. They are life! The enemy does not have authority to take our lives prematurely, as long as we walk under the covering of the King.

The Presence

I have just reread the biography of Bilquis Sheikh, a highborn Pakistani woman who became a believer in Jesus and risked her life and everything she held dear in order to express her faith in Jesus through baptism.[3] Madame Sheikh had read Psalm 91, and she walked in an amazing sense of the Lord's Presence. She knew that Muslims who come to faith in Jesus are often killed for defaming the family honor. Her house was not well protected from intruders, and most of her servants had left their posts out of fear from reprisals for even working for her.

Madame Sheikh's Christian friends began to urge her to put heavy metal grilles over her doors and windows. She agreed to the idea reluctantly and started for the phone to call a repairman, only to realize that "the Presence" had lifted.

She paused, pondered, prayed . . . and remembered.

Not only did she then refuse to have the doors and windows barred, but she dismissed her servants to their own quarters at nightfall each evening, entrusting herself to the Lord, whom she was following. She had read Psalm 91, and she believed it.

A few mornings ago I awoke with a message emblazoned on my heart, a message I sent to some of those with whom I walk most closely.

"We do not want simply to make it Home ourselves," I told them. "We want to take millions with us." I saw a picture of a gigantic storm, but we were walking *into* the storm, not *away* from it. We were walking forward to rescue those who were perishing.

Another message flashed across my screen: "When the storms come, don't head for the bunker with your food and your guns to hide from the approaching disasters. Move into the storms, assured of His divine protection as long as you are in His will."

Learn to distinguish between the voices.

The voices of the ten spies remind us only of the problems. The voices of Caleb and Joshua acknowledge the seriousness of the battle but point us to the victory. Let us not only be careful to listen to the Calebs and Joshuas of our day but also *become* those Calebs and Joshuas!

"We should go up and take possession of the land, for we can certainly do it. . . . Do not be afraid. . . . The Lord is with us." I promised in the introduction to remind you of this: The Lord is with us, so there is no need for fear. He will work out everything for our good.

3

Expect the Harvests

"The time to reap has come, for the harvest of the earth is ripe."

Revelation 14:15

Our world is not a safe place. Multiple millions have been killed during the wars, persecutions, religious purging and imprisonments of the 20th and 21st centuries.

Joseph Stalin's reign was responsible for an estimated twenty million deaths of those who would not allow the Soviet leader to become their god.

Adolf Hitler and his National Socialist loyalists are credited with another twelve million, six million of them Jewish people who were murdered in the gas ovens of Auschwitz, Birkenau and other horrifying death machines.

Communist China is thought to have killed upward of fifty million people between 1949 and 1969, with millions more—especially Christians who refused to abide by the limits of the state-approved form of Christianity—being imprisoned and tortured. When a small group of us smuggled Bibles into China in October 1989, only a few months following the brutal attack of the student uprising, bloodstains were still visible on the pavement of Tiananmen Square in Beijing.

One and a half million died in Ethiopia after Christian Emperor Haile Selassie was killed and Communist ruler Mengistu Haile Mariam came to power.

Ruthless henchman Idi Amin left Uganda bankrupt, with hundreds of thousands dead and many more having fled their homes during his evil reign in the 1970s.

Many North Korean believers lost their lives during the tyrannical rule of Communist leaders in their land. The March 22, 2014, edition of *World* magazine devotes eight pages to a story chronicling the torture, abuse, imprisonment and deaths of thousands of North Koreans who dare to express their belief in Jesus.[1] Thousands of others still live under the daily threat of persecution, as do those who have come to faith in much of the Middle East, Indonesia and other nations that have no freedom of religious expression.

Taliban, Hezbollah, Hamas, al Qaeda, Muslim Brotherhood and ISIS spread fear throughout the world. The dream of an Arab Spring became a nightmare of greater violence. Just a few years ago in a suburb of Cairo, radical Islamists overtook a mosque for the purpose of rounding up and torturing Christians who were demonstrating against the ruling Muslim Brotherhood.

Coptic Christians face the daily threats of intimidation, rape and torture. "Accept Islam or be killed," they are warned. In 2014 the world media was filled not only with reports of the publicly televised beheadings of "infidels" from the West but also with reports of children murdered before their parents' eyes if they did not accept Islam.

After the overthrow of Muammar Gaddafi in Libya, Christians in Benghazi continue to be jailed, tortured or killed for sharing their faith. "[They] are being treated similarly to [Libyan] blacks, who since the rebel uprising have been rounded up in their thousands, detained and tortured to death in prison camps merely on the accusation that they worked for Gaddafi, in a barbarous act of ethnic cleansing."[2]

Sister Agnes Mariam, the founder of a monastery in Qara, Syria, has lived in that country since 1994. Some of us were privileged to visit with Sister Agnes in a meeting in Turkey in 2006. In an interview on Alex Jones' Prison Planet, she spoke openly of the disappointment among believers who had assumed that life under Bashar al-Assad would be better, only to find that Christians suffered even more intense persecution under the West-backed rebels. Hundreds of thousands of believers lost their lives in the ensuing years.

In October 1991 I flew with a couple of my friends to Kano, Nigeria, to join Reinhard Bonnke in one of his evangelistic campaigns. We circled the airfield for some minutes before we were given clearance for landing. Then we were whisked away to a secure location because of radical Muslim uprisings that ultimately caused the cancellation of the meetings. For the entire three days of our brief visit, we stayed in a secluded hideout under police protection. In the dark of night we were taken to the airport, which remained closed until all of us could be evacuated. We learned later that more than two hundred of those who were preparing for the evangelistic meetings had been killed, and that the angry mob was on its way to our hideout as we were being hurried to the airport.

Attack on America

Since the advent of suicide bombers, no place in the world is secure. This became painfully evident to Americans in the attacks of September 11, 2001. As the four hijacked jets raced toward their targets, I was at Abraham's Well near Beersheba in Israel. When the report of the first strike was relayed to us, some of our small group wondered if this could possibly be pilot error. Nothing like this had ever occurred in the United States. The second attack, also against the World Trade Center, left no doubt that our nation was under siege.

Our group drove back to Jerusalem, listening intently to additional news regarding the other two jets and wondering if the West would finally understand the daily threat commonplace to Israel, where suicide bombers stalk malls, schools, restaurants, buses and homes.

Bold headlines in the *Jerusalem Post* the next morning announced: "America under Attack: Thousands die as two hijacked planes destroy World Trade Center." Almost the whole front page of one of the Hebrew language newspapers showed the two towers engulfed in flames. The English headlines read: "We Stand with You, America."

For a day or two following 9/11, God was welcomed back into the public sector and even into American schools, though in 1962 our government had evicted Him by disallowing prayer in classrooms.

Good News

But we have been concentrating on bad news, and bad news demoralizes. Good news energizes. We were not created to be driven by fear, but to live by faith and to have hope.

This is why Paul, writing from a Roman jail, told the believers to "Rejoice!" (Philippians 4:4) and not to be "anxious about anything," that peace beyond all comprehension will invade our hearts and our minds if we continue to pray from a point of rejoicing in what God has done and from a heart full of thanksgiving (see Philippians 4:6–7).

Paul's body may have been in a dungeon, but his heart was full of hope. Why? He lived what he taught. He did not spend time concentrating on the bad news, but on the glorious thought that the Good News of Jesus was being spread about, even among the Roman guards (see Philippians 1:13). "Concentrate on things that are true, noble, right, pure, lovely, admirable and excellent," he instructed his fellow travelers (see Philippians 4:8).

So I want to be a Caleb, a Joshua, and talk about the amazing conquests of God's army that are taking place in the very midst of the horror.

Our God Is Greater

"You come against me with sword and spear and javelin," young David told Goliath, "but I come against you in the name of the LORD Almighty, the God of the armies of Israel, whom you have defied. This day the LORD will deliver you into my hands" (1 Samuel 17:45–46). Communism, radical Islam, radical Hinduism and all the other enemies of God may come against us with imprisonment, beatings and even death, but we will come to them with forgiveness and love and redemption through the name, the authority, the blood and the power of Jesus.

Like our predecessors Caleb and Joshua, we will go forward in strength. You will not hear good reports from electronic media or on the evening news. To receive this kind of encouragement, you need to read reports from organizations like Youth With A Mission or the Center for World Missions or the Voice of the Martyrs, or hear directly from those who are fighting the battles and experiencing the victories.

The Chinese revival has energized mission intercessors since the first reports of the growing house church movement reached the ears of the Western community of believers. About the same time that Israel became a nation, China adopted Communist rule. The persecution of believers was so severe that many feared for the survival of any expression of faith in Jesus in that vast nation. Yet by the time of Israel's Jubilee celebration fifty years later, reports were leaked that the number of Chinese believers had increased to eighty million or more. Today the number is still advancing by thirty thousand or more a day.[3]

In 2012 my colleague Tod McDowell was in Kansas City with a group of leaders from the underground Church in China. He was privileged to speak to them regarding their "Back to Jerusalem" movement. Not only did he encourage them in their vision to take the Good News of Jesus from the eastern provinces of China westward toward Jerusalem, reaching the Muslim, Buddhist and Hindu nations in between, but he also challenged them to go into the very nation from which our salvation originated. As Tod began sharing with these Chinese brothers and mentioned the one hundred twenty million believers in China, one of the leaders spoke up with a gentle correction: "One hundred *forty* million!" (Since then, estimates are as high as one hundred seventy million.)

My heart still warms every time I think of the stories from Brother Danyun, who traveled by bicycle through several Chinese provinces to collect stories of the revival.[4]

I will never forget the account of the widowed mother who was arrested and imprisoned for her faith, leaving her three young children at home to be cared for by fellow believers. When she was first incarcerated, she knew of only one other believer among the hundreds of inmates. Eight years later, when she was released, more than half the prison population and many of the guards had come to faith. As she left the prison gates, she wept over leaving her flock behind.

Among the photos on my iPhone, I still have the picture of Brother Yun, the so-called "heavenly man," whom I met briefly in Jerusalem; later both Tod and I met him in Nashville. His legs had been intentionally broken so that he would have no hope of escape. But God had a different plan. Brother Yun experienced a Peter-type deliverance when the Lord told him to get up on his broken legs and walk out of the prison. He obeyed, walking out of his cell through three prison gates that were inexplicably opened, past guards whose eyes were blinded to his escape, only to find that there was a taxi waiting at the prison entrance. From there he was taken to a friend's house, from which he escaped to the West. Also like Peter, not until he was outside the prison walls was he sure he was not living in a dream or a vision.

I will also always remember Brother Yun's confession that it is often harder to live radically for the Lord in the Western world than in the detention and concentration camps of China. It is easy in our soft culture to be lulled into complacent lives of comfort and compromise.

Though today some areas of China face less persecution, reports speak of an increase of harassment, oppression and persecution in other sections of the nation.[5]

Ten Million Bibles—in Iran

The Chinese revival is not the only astonishing surprise from the persecuted Church. I first found out about the revival in Iran through *Mission Frontiers*, a magazine that serves the Center for World Missions. The article began with the consensus of Iran's national cabinet concerning the growing Christ-ward movement spreading through the nation: "The only way were [sic] going to stop them is to kill them."[6]

The modern revival began in the early 1960s when a team of American missionaries began to devote themselves to the Persian-Armenian community in Tehran. One of their first disciples was a man named Haik Hovsepian, who was later assassinated for his faith. By the time of his death in 1994, this Christ-ward movement was out of control. There was great unrest, especially among young people. These young people were searching for truth and were convinced that the truth was not to be found in government control. When the government began confiscating Bibles, many of the young people became determined to possess one themselves. It was estimated, at the time of this article, that ten million Bibles would not supply the demand. One believer reported that she had personally distributed twenty thousand Bibles and had never had anyone turn down her offer.

Christian satellite TV programs have become popular and are viewed through satellite dishes that were smuggled illegally into Iran by some of the very government officials who had outlawed them. It is believed that seventy percent of the country is now watching Christian television. At the time of the article, the number of believers had reached a million or more. Some of those Iranian believers with whom I have personally spoken report that revival has now reached seven million or more.

Jew-Hating Muslim Finds True Path of Peace

One young man with whom I visited on Skype had come to Ukraine because he had no hope of studying medicine in Iran. Though he had been raised as a devout Muslim and a radical hater of Jewish people, when he moved to Kiev, for some reason that he himself could not fully explain, he began attending a large Messianic congregation led by Boris Grisenko. He became a serious God-seeker.

One morning at the conclusion of the assembly, my friend noticed an older woman sitting behind him, praying. The Lord nudged him: *Go ask her to pray for you.* He cautiously approached the woman with his request.

The woman began to weep. "The Lord told me that a young Muslim man would approach me this morning and ask for prayer," she told him.

My formerly angry, Jew-hating friend had a transformation of heart that morning, a transformation that set him on a path of peace. My own relationship with him came when he showed an interest in translating my book *Your People Shall Be My People* into Farsi (later into Arabic as well). We placed the book on the Internet, to be downloaded without cost so that any Farsi-speaking Iranians, either in their homeland or scattered abroad, would have access to a book that shows the connection between Israel coming to know their Messiah and the awakening to faith among the nations.

Another of my Farsi-speaking Iranian friends was reared in a devout Muslim family in Iran. His mother died when he was four years old, and he became sorely depressed for the next years of his life, a depression that also expressed itself in stuttering so badly that he could not carry on a normal conversation.

By the age of twelve, after a number of other deaths in the family and no forthcoming answers to his constant barrage of questions about God, about death and about life after death, his father enrolled him in the finest Muslim academy in the city.

"Teach this young man about Allah," the father instructed. "Help him memorize the Koran."

So Amiel began memorizing the Koran and learning about Allah. But there was still a great void in Amiel's heart. He began to go to a library and search for books about other faiths—Hinduism, Buddhism and other religions—but nothing seemed to remove the weight inside his heart. One day he asked a woman working in the library if she had a Bible.

A secret believer in Jesus, she smiled and told him kindly, "No, we do not have a Bible." She later found one and gave it to him.

Amiel began reading his Bible immediately. He was captivated by the story of the real God who loved His people but who also punished disobedience. Soon he came to the story of Jesus, and much to his astonishment, without even knowing when it occurred, he realized that the weight in his heart had lifted and that he could carry on a conversation without stuttering. Almost involuntarily he had begun to believe that Jesus is God's answer and, therefore, had no difficulty surrendering his life to Him.

The love of Jesus will always conquer hatred. Paul said, "Christ's love compels us" (2 Corinthians 5:14). "Love your enemies, do good to those who hate you" was Jesus' own admonition (Luke 6:27).

A Jihadist Who Found Jesus

One of the most difficult places for this love to penetrate may be among the Palestinian terrorists. They have been reared with such intense hatred toward the Jewish people and Christians that they would appear to be impossible to reach. Not so. There are now a number of former terrorists who are bringing their message of love and hope to the world.

One of them is Tass Saada, whose story is told in the book *Once an Arafat Man*.[7] Tass was born in Gaza and raised in Saudi Arabia in a world of radical Islam and violent Palestinian nationalism. During his teen years he became a personal friend of Yasser Arafat. By his own admission he was a killer. He murdered Jews, whether civilians or soldiers. He attacked Christians, sometimes tossing hand grenades into their homes; at other times strafing them with machine-gun fire.

In the foreword to Tass's book, Joel Rosenberg calls him a "jihadist who found Jesus, a violent revolutionary who was radically transformed one day by the power of the Holy Spirit and became a man of peace and compassion." Rosenberg then declares, "This is the story of the greatness of our great God. It is the story of a man who fell in love with a Savior who loves Arabs as well as Jews."[8]

Most remarkable things happen when we meet Jesus. Joel spoke of the day he and Tass met. "Here we were, a former aide to PLO Chairman Yasser Arafat and a former aide to Prime Minister Benjamin Netanyahu, hugging each other—not trying to kill each other—in the heart of Jerusalem. All because of the work Jesus had done to give us hearts of love rather than hatred."[9]

I witnessed a similar encounter of another Tass and another Joel one day while visiting Gateways Beyond training school in Cyprus. The room was packed with worshipers, both Jewish and from the nations. I was standing close to the back when a young Arab entered the room and walked over to David Rudolph, the leader of the school.

"Is that an Israeli over there?" the young man asked.

"Yes," was David's response.

"I need to wash his feet."

And so, before the entire room full of 75 or 80 of us from the nations, Samer, a former Palestinian terrorist from Lebanon, walked over to Heskel, an officer in the Israel Defense Force, and washed his feet. I cannot read stories like those from Tass and Joel without a smile on my face.

Yes, this is the age when wickedness is increasing, but it is also the age in which righteousness is conquering wickedness. This is a day in which to be encouraged, not to be dismayed. This is a time when we must remember that all things, yes, *all things*, work for our good if we will keep loving the Lord and stay in the calling.

4

Remember the Passover

"Remember this day."

Exodus 13:3 NASB

I became more acutely aware of the significance of Passover during the Jesus Movement of the late '60s and '70s, when Jewish hippies often became "Jesus freaks" and began to discover the Jewishness of Jesus.

What an intriguing time to be alive! Young people I knew who often had little orientation to anything of God were coming to faith, hungry to know more. Newly acquired Bibles, wrapped in handmade cloth or leather covers, were in abundance. Parks, storefronts, dorm rooms, flop houses and street corners served as classrooms. The nearby Little Harpeth River, just south of Nashville, became our large baptismal pool. Swimming pools and bathtubs also worked quite well.

Still on the faculty at one of our city's Christian colleges and dressed in my fashionable knit suit, I would often leave campus, drive to the river with the new believers, take off shoes and socks to become the baptizer, then drive back to the campus. By the time

I arrived for an afternoon class, only the bottom part of my trousers indicated any unusual activity in which I had been involved! Many church attendees found the dress of the hippies-turned-Jesus-freaks and their passion for the things of God to be incongruous. Church leaders faced a dilemma in their congregational and business meetings: Enforce the dress code "appropriate" for the house of God, meaning suits and ties, which could drive away the enthusiastic new converts, or agree to their unwelcome bare and dusty feet on the plush carpets.

I will never forget one evening in a storefront Bible study I taught when one of our fresh disciples, clad in T-shirt and tattered jeans, rushed toward me, grinning jubilantly. "I read the whole book of Revelation last night!"

I was somewhat stunned since the account of John's apocalyptic visions was, in my estimation, not the best place for a new believer to begin to understand Scripture.

Suppressing my judgmental thoughts and trying to keep a straight face, I asked, "What did you learn?"

Exuberantly, my young friend announced, "Evil always loses and good always wins!"

Wow! He got it! I thought, in my best hippie-expressed internal pondering. That really is the message of Revelation. From beginning to end, John urges all future disciples to become passionate followers of Jesus so that they can avoid the plagues and destruction of the future and enter triumphantly into their intended destiny. John serves us in much the same capacity as Moses and Aaron served Israel during the Passover exodus: "Keep the faith during difficult times; we're getting out of here."

The Ultimate Passover

I call John's apocalyptic visions a depiction of the "ultimate Passover." First, there is a description of how difficult things are among God's people in a foreign land (the letters to the seven churches of Asia). Then the scene changes to describe God's victory Lamb, whose blood releases us from slavery and ushers us into a secure and confident future. As the story unfolds, there are plagues and a Pharaoh-type opponent with his alarming and intimidating team. God's people experience some of the horror, but are ultimately delivered and sing the song of Moses and the Lamb (see Revelation 15:3). I began to understand why the modern-day Jewish believers were so fascinated with the apostolic writings. Their own Scriptures were coming alive in Jesus/Yeshua, the Lamb of God, the fulfillment of their prophetic feasts.

The Passover celebration is the annual day of remembrance that calls Jewish people back to their heritage. "Next year in Jerusalem!" is heralded even among Jewish families who either never have been or never intend to go. The Passover is a sort of clarion call to Jewish people to remember their roots.

John's Revelation serves much the same purpose. As the seals are opened and the trumpets sound, John calls God's people to repentance. John is the voice of Moses and Aaron, trying to convince Israel not to let the hard times deceive or deter. Victory is ahead.

For hundreds of years before their exodus, Israel lived in a land that was not their intended homeland, just as we do. Life was hard, as is ours, even in the best of lives. Through all those years of history in Egypt, God's people knew of the promises about their homeland, but the memory held no commanding influence on their humdrum lives. This is not unlike a great majority of believers, at least in the Western world, where the promises of God often pale in the face of much activity and the disappointments of daily living.

The message of Revelation, like many of the prophetic words describing the future, becomes even more relevant as we see what happened to Israel just before their release. When Moses and his brother, Aaron, went to the elders of Israel announcing their soon exodus, and the Israelites "heard that the LORD was concerned about them and had seen their misery, they bowed down and worshiped" (Exodus 4:31).

But as that message began to play out in their enslaved lives, rather than rejoicing because the end was near, they became enraged against the very people who were leading them into victory. The days just prior to Israel's release proved to be the most intense time of suffering in all of their history. Now not only were they required to produce their quota of bricks for their Egyptian taskmasters, but they had to find their own straw with which to make them (see Exodus 5:6–9).

To make matters worse, the first confrontations between the forces of good and evil were not overly convincing. The magicians of Egypt performed the same miracles that God's representatives produced.

Is this not what Jesus was saying when He told His disciples that, in the future, "false messiahs and false prophets will appear and perform great signs and wonders" (Matthew 24:24)?

Notice that Jesus did not say that they will *seem* to perform miracles, but that they will actually perform great miracles. This will not be unlike the time of the original Passover, when the magicians of the Pharaoh were able to turn their own rods into snakes (even though Moses' rod swallowed up their rods), turn water to blood and cause frogs to come up out of the Nile. This was *real* power, not just an optical illusion.

In John's picture, the beast out of the sea

performed great signs, even causing fire to come down from heaven to the earth in full view of the people. Because of the signs it was given power to perform on behalf of the first beast, it deceived the inhabitants of the earth. It ordered them to set up an image in honor of the beast who was wounded by the sword and yet lived. The second beast was given power to give breath to the image of the first beast, so that the image could speak and cause all who refused to worship the image to be killed.

Revelation 13:13–15

Fire from heaven! Breath to an idol! This from the enemy of God! These are dangerous times. No wonder John cries in the middle of his vision, "This calls for patient endurance and faithfulness on the part of God's people. . . . This calls for wisdom!" (Revelation 13:10, 18).

Do you see why the message of this book is so important for our end time generation? The enemy will exhibit great power; thus, we must become so filled with God's Spirit that we can discern the source of that power and stand with confidence in Jesus' presence just as did Stephen and other great martyrs of the faith.

Even as I write this I am remembering an older acquaintance of mine whose eyesight had dimmed so that he was almost blind. He had been to medical doctors, and he had asked Christians to pray for him, but nothing had helped. So he was ready to turn to other powers. He learned of an occult leader in the Philippines who had documented cases of healing. My friend was willing to submit to a foreign power in order to gain the victory that he so desperately wanted.

Though he was seriously tempted, he did not go. The real danger would have come had he gone and his sight been restored: He might have been tempted to turn to the occult rather than remain faithful to Jesus. Better to remain blind for a season than to resort to the powers of the enemy that may indeed heal but lead us away from the Eternal One.

The Invincible Ones

As in the Passover story, John lets us know that only after we have passed through a season of intense adversity/tribulation will we become the invincible ones. Those who have God's "seal on the foreheads" (Revelation 7:3) are protected from the enemy.

"Fall on us and hide us from the face of him who sits on the throne and from the wrath of the Lamb! For the great day of their wrath has come" (Revelation 6:16–17) is the cry heard when the sixth seal is opened. Though Jesus did not describe seals being opened in heaven, He warned us to expect the kinds of conditions John describes in the seals: war, famine, pestilence, natural disasters and death.

Following the breaking of the seventh seal, John sees seven angels being given seven trumpets. When the trumpets are sounded, the angels release plagues upon the earth: hail, water to blood and other disasters reminiscent of ancient Israel's experience before her release. John specifically calls these manifestations *plagues*—"the rest of mankind who were not killed by these plagues . . ." (Revelation 9:20).

That is why the Passover story is so encouraging to me. Israel was in Egypt; we are in our own Egypt. The Israelites experienced the hardest season of their lives before the deliverance, just as I believe we will. But they were spared the last plagues, even though they were still present in Egypt when those plagues were released.

Watch how all this developed as described in Exodus 7:14–11:10.

> *Plague #1: Water to blood.* Israel must have experienced this. There is no mention that they were spared from the same horror that befell all of Egypt.
>
> *Plague #2: Frogs.* Same thing. An Israelite had to be a strong believer to endure this one without complaining, trusting that God indeed was in the process of delivering them, though they did not understand.
>
> *Plague #3: Gnats.* Up until this time the Egyptian magicians were able to produce the same miracles as Moses

and Aaron. But this time, "when the magicians tried to produce gnats by their secret arts, they could not [and said to Pharaoh], 'This is the finger of God'" (Exodus 8:18–19). At this point, things changed for Israel. They were still in the land of Egypt, but they did not experience the plagues of Egypt. Notice how the biblical chronicler records the change.

Plague #4: Flies. "On that day I will deal differently with the land of Goshen, where my people live; no swarms of flies will be there" (Exodus 8:22).

Plague #5: Death of livestock. "The LORD will make a distinction between the livestock of Israel and that of Egypt, so that no animal belonging to the Israelites will die" (Exodus 9:4).

Plague #6: Boils. "Festering boils will break out on people and animals" (Exodus 9:9). Though there is no specific mention this time between Egypt and Israel, the principle has been established and continues with the remaining plagues.

Plague #7: Hail. "The only place it did not hail was the land of Goshen, where the Israelites were" (Exodus 9:26).

Plague #8: Locusts. "They will devour what little you have left after the hail. . . . They will fill your houses and those of all your officials and all the Egyptians" (Exodus 10:5–6).

Plague #9: Darkness. "Total darkness covered all Egypt for three days. No one could see anyone else or move about for three days. Yet all the Israelites had light in the places where they lived" (Exodus 10:22–23).

Plague #10: Death of the firstborn. Not only was the last plague a judgment upon Egypt and her gods, but the application of lambs' blood on the Israelites' doorframes foreshadowed another Lamb who would be slain, and whose blood would be stroked across human hearts for an eternal deliverance from the slavery and bondage that has engulfed Adam's children since that day in the Garden. Not surprising then that when Jesus' cousin John saw Jesus coming toward him, he cried out, "Look, the Lamb of God, who takes away the sin of the world!" (John 1:29). Perhaps John was reminded of words from the Torah: "It is the blood that makes atonement for one's life" (Leviticus 17:11).

The Blood of the Lamb

John the Baptizer knew what he was saying. This Man to whom he was pointing is the fulfillment of every Passover lamb killed through all the centuries. Once His blood was given there was no longer any need for the slaughter of animals. It seems that God was so intent on getting that message across to the Jewish people and to the whole world that He allowed the Temple in Jerusalem to be destroyed a few years later, after which no further lambs have been sacrificed.

John the apostle picks up on the Passover story as he refers several times to Jesus as the Lamb of God who "has freed us from our sins by his blood" (Revelation 1:5). In describing the scene in heaven when the Lamb takes the scroll from the hand of Him who sits upon the throne, John tells how the four living creatures and the 24 elders sing a new song as they fall down in worship: "You are worthy to take the scroll and to open its seals, because you were slain, and with your blood you purchased for God persons from every tribe and language and people and nation" (Revelation 5:9).

Then all of heaven and earth breaks out in praise.

"Worthy is the Lamb, who was slain, to receive power and wealth and wisdom and strength and honor and glory and praise! . . . To him who sits on the throne and to the Lamb be praise and honor and glory and power, for ever and ever!"

Revelation 5:12–13

Overcomers are victorious because "they have washed their robes and made them white in the blood of the Lamb" (Revelation 7:14). The blood of the Lamb secures our victory (see Revelation 12:11), and when this Revelation/Passover epic reaches its zenith, the Rider on the white horse is seen descending from heaven with the armies of heaven following, His "robe dipped in blood" (Revelation 19:13).

What is the message of the Passover? What is the message from John's Revelation? What is this message that is so relevant for us today? Tough times are coming, but hold on.

The best is yet ahead.

5

Pay Attention
to God's Calendar

"These are my appointed festivals, the appointed festivals of the LORD, which you are to proclaim as sacred assemblies."

Leviticus 23:2

Many people will be surprised to know that Jesus was not crucified on Good Friday, nor was He raised to life on Easter Sunday. Rather, He was crucified on the eve of Passover (*Pesach*) and was raised to life on the Festival of First Fruits (*HaBikkurim*), two of "the LORD's appointed festivals" (Leviticus 23:4). These feast days rarely coincide with the traditional Christian calendar.

Yes, *Easter* is mentioned in Acts 12:4 in the King James Version, but this is an unfortunate and inaccurate translation of the Greek word for *Passover*, a word that is translated *Passover* in every other accepted version of Scripture.[1]

God's Calendar

During Creation week, God said, "Let there be lights in the vault of the sky to separate the day from the night, and *let them serve as signs to mark sacred times, and days and years*" (Genesis 1:14, emphasis added). The psalmist affirmed the Genesis account by acknowledging: "He made the moon to mark the seasons" (Psalm 104:19).

God's calendar is based on a lunar month and a solar year, with each new moon announcing the arrival of a new month, the full moon always arriving on the fourteenth day of the lunar month. To keep the nation attuned to His calendar, God instructed Israel to blow the silver trumpets on each new moon (see Numbers 10:1, 10).

Since recognizing this, I find my attention drawn repeatedly to the phases of the moon. If I see a new moon, I know that this is the first day of one of God's biblical months. If I see a full moon in late March or April, then I am looking at the Passover moon. Passover is always on the fourteenth day of Aviv, the Hebrew word for "spring." The month later came to be called Nisan (see Nehemiah 2:1; Esther 3:7).

Passover month marks the beginning of God's calendar year. God gave Moses and Aaron this instruction as they were leaving Egypt: "This month is to be for you the first month, the first month of your year" (Exodus 12:2). He also told them: "Today, in the month of Aviv, you are leaving" (13:4). "Observe the month of Aviv and celebrate the Passover of the LORD your God, because in the month of Aviv he brought you out of Egypt by night" (Deuteronomy 16:1).[2]

The Spring Festivals—His Sacrifice

The festivals of the Lord are celebrations of the goodness of the Lord, remembering His Presence among His people, but they

62

are also given to us as a prophetic picture of His first advent and His coming return.

The spring festivals found astonishing fulfillment in Jesus' life when He was among us. He was executed on Passover and raised on the Festival of First Fruits. His sinless life is symbolized through the Festival of Unleavened Bread, and He poured out His Spirit on Pentecost.

Watch how carefully the spring feasts unfolded in His life.

Passover

Passover is all about the deliverance from slavery that came to Israel through the blood of lambs. As we have noted, John the Baptist spoke prophetically about the purpose of Jesus' life that day when Jesus was approaching him: "Look, the Lamb of God who takes away the sin of the world!"

Isaiah had prophesied that the coming Messiah would be "led like a lamb to the slaughter, and as a sheep before its shearers is silent, so he did not open his mouth" (Isaiah 53:7). Matthew described the perfect fulfillment of that prophecy when Jesus was brought before Pilate with all the accusations from the Jewish leaders, but "made no reply, not even to a single charge—to the great amazement of the governor" (Matthew 27:14).

But there is more. Every family in Israel was directed to select the Passover sacrifice on the tenth day of Nisan. They were to examine the lamb during the next four days to be sure that he was flawless and, therefore, an appropriate offering to the Lord.

> "Tell the whole community of Israel that on the tenth day of this month each man is to take a lamb for his family, one for each household," [God told Moses]. . . . "Take care of them until the fourteenth day of the month, when all the members of the community of Israel must slaughter them at twilight.

Then they are to take some of the blood and put it on the sides and tops of the doorframes of the houses where they eat the lambs."

Exodus 12:3, 6–7

Notice how the events of those last four days played out, leading up to Jesus' death.

John tells us that six days before the Passover, thus, the ninth day of Nisan, Jesus arrived in Bethany. The next day, the tenth day of Nisan, He entered Jerusalem from the Mount of Olives in what has come to be known as the Triumphal Entry (see John 12:1, 12). Upon that eventful arrival, "the Pharisees said to one another, 'See, this is getting us nowhere. Look how the whole world has gone after him!'" (John 12:19). They then "schemed to arrest Jesus secretly and kill him" (Matthew 26:4).

God's perfect Lamb was thus selected on the tenth day of Nisan, just as the Scripture had prescribed.

What happened for the next four days? He was examined by Annas, the Sanhedrin, Caiaphas, Herod and Pilate.

Annas: "The soldiers . . . brought him first to Annas . . . [who] questioned Jesus about his disciples and his teaching" (John 18:12–13, 19).

The Sanhedrin: "They took Jesus to the high priest, and all the chief priests, the elders and the teachers of the law came together. . . . The chief priests and the whole Sanhedrin were looking for evidence against Jesus" (Mark 14:53, 55).

Caiaphas: "Tell us if you are the Messiah, the Son of God" (Matthew 26:63).

Pilate: "Are you the king of the Jews?" (Matthew 27:11).

Herod: "He plied [Jesus] with many questions" (Luke 23:9).

After all the questions, what were Pilate's last words? "I find no basis for a charge against this man" (Luke 23:4). In other words, "He has been properly examined, and no flaw has been found in Him. He is a worthy sacrifice."

Jesus was then nailed to the execution stake at nine o'clock on the morning of the thirteenth day of Nisan and died six hours later, at three in the afternoon. When the soldiers came to take Him down from the cross, they did not break his legs, as they did the legs of the two men on the adjoining crosses. Instead, they pierced His side so that blood flowed from the wound at the precise time that the blood from other lambs was flowing throughout Jerusalem.

To Corinth, Paul wrote, "Christ, our Passover lamb, has been sacrificed" (1 Corinthians 5:7).

The Festival of First Fruits

The Festival of First Fruits is observed three days after Passover—"on the day after the Sabbath" (Leviticus 23:11). "Bring to the priest a sheaf of the first grain you harvest," was God's instruction (Leviticus 23:10). The priest was to "wave the sheaf" (Leviticus 23:12) in gratitude before the Lord and as a proclamation of the greater harvest ahead.

Jesus is our first fruits offering. He was raised to life on the Festival of First Fruits, His resurrected body a sheaf offering proclamation, pointing forward to all who would one day be raised from the dead.

Paul told the Corinthians,

> If Christ has not been raised, your faith is futile. . . . But Christ has indeed been raised from the dead, the firstfruits of those who have fallen asleep. . . . For as in Adam all die, so in Christ all will be made alive. But each in turn: Christ, the firstfruits; then, when he comes, those who belong to him.
>
> 1 Corinthians 15:17, 20, 22–23

The Festival of Unleavened Bread

The Festival of Unleavened Bread begins on the fifteenth day of Nisan, the day after Passover, and lasts seven days. "For seven days you must eat bread made without yeast" (Leviticus 23:6).

Why a feast of unleavened bread? First of all, this is an experiential remembrance of Israel's rapid departure from Egypt and the admonition to all to be ready to depart at any time. "Eat it in haste; it is the LORD's Passover," God told Israel (Exodus 12:11).

But this is also a reminder of our deliverance from a life of sin, since leaven is a symbol of sin. I like to think of it this way: Leavened bread pretends to be more bread than it really is. Like sin, much of it is empty air.

Paul challenged the believers at Corinth, "Get rid of the old yeast, so that you may be a new unleavened batch—as you really are. . . . Keep the Festival, not with the old bread leavened with malice and wickedness, but with the unleavened bread of sincerity and truth" (1 Corinthians 5:7–8).

Pentecost

Pentecost, occurring fifty days after Passover, is the last of the spring festivals, a day when Israel celebrates the giving of the Law on Mount Sinai. For those of us who are followers of Jesus, it is also the annual celebration of the outpouring of the Holy Spirit on that Pentecost morning following Jesus' ascension.

Shortly before His departure Jesus told His disciples, "Do not leave Jerusalem, but wait for the gift my Father promised. . . . In a few days you will be baptized with the Holy Spirit. . . . You will receive power when the Holy Spirit comes on you" (Acts 1:4–5, 8).

So "when the day of Pentecost came . . . all of them were filled with the Holy Spirit" (Acts 2:1, 4). Peter told the assembled crowd, "The promise [of the Holy Spirit] is for you and your children and for all who are far off—for all whom the Lord our God will call" (Acts 2:39).

The Fall Festivals—His Return

The fall feasts—the Festival of Trumpets, the Day of Atonement and the Festival of Tabernacles—will find their greatest fulfillment when Jesus comes again.

Between the spring feasts and the fall feasts is a long interval, the prophetic interval in which we now find ourselves. After the spring planting and the summer of growth, the time arrives to gather the final harvest and celebrate.

The Festival of Trumpets

The Festival of Trumpets is the first of these fall feasts. It occurs on the first day of the seventh month—the month of Tishrei—and is referred to as *Yom Teruah*, which means the "Day of Blowing" (see Leviticus 23:24; Numbers 29:1). In the Jewish community this festival is commonly called *Rosh Hashanah* (Head of the Year) and is celebrated as the beginning of the New Year, but this is not its biblical designation. Each festival was established as a sacred assembly requiring all Jewish males to gather in Jerusalem. After the long summer months without any festivals, the Festival of Trumpets is a call to the nation to come and prepare for the arrival of the holiest day on the calendar, the Day of Atonement, and the final Festival of Tabernacles.

The Day of Atonement

The Day of Atonement was the only day of the year when the high priest entered into the Holy of Holies, an annual day of judgment when the priest made an atoning sacrifice to cleanse himself and the people from sin. Jesus, as our High Priest, has already "entered the Most Holy Place once for all by his own blood. . . . For by one sacrifice he has made perfect forever those who are being made holy" (Hebrews 9:12, 10:14). But there is yet a day coming when all will be "judged according to what they [have] done as recorded in the books" (Revelation 20:12).

The Festival of Tabernacles

The Festival of Tabernacles is an annual remembrance of God's supernatural provisions and Presence during the forty years the Israelites wandered in the wilderness. For us, it is a wistful yearning for the day when "God's dwelling place is now among the people, and he will dwell with them. They will be his people, and God himself will be with them and be their God" (Revelation 21:3).

Interesting that during the millennial reign of Jesus, the Festival of Tabernacles will be used to call the nations to repentance. Zechariah says,

> "The survivors from all the nations that have attacked Jerusalem will go up year after year to worship the King, the LORD Almighty, and to celebrate the Festival of Tabernacles. If any of the peoples of the earth do not go up to Jerusalem to worship the King, the LORD Almighty, they will have no rain."
>
> Zechariah 14:16–17

Paul understood the prophetic significance of the fall feasts when he wrote, "We will all be changed—in a flash, in the twinkling of an eye, at the last trumpet" (1 Corinthians 15:51–52). "The Lord himself will come down from heaven, with a loud command, with the voice of the archangel and with the trumpet call of God, and the dead in Christ will rise first" (1 Thessalonians 4:16).

The Sabbath

No description of God's festivals is complete without referring to the Sabbath. The Genesis account of Creation tells us, "God blessed the seventh day and made it holy, because on it he rested from all the work of creating that he had done" (Genesis 2:3). Thus, the Sabbath was made holy at Creation. No wonder then, when God gave Moses the Ten Commandments, He said, "Remember the Sabbath day by keeping it holy" (Exodus 20:8). Israel was asked to *keep* holy what God had called holy in the Garden of His creation.

The Western world seems to take pride in working long hours and often seven days a week, but God has ordained a day of rest, a day of declaring through our actions that our God is not a slave driver. He will care for us if we take a day each week to rest, to seek Him, to rejoice with family and friends, to refresh.

Yes, God has a calendar, and we have a calendar. Though we are grateful for all those who throughout the centuries and throughout the world have continued to honor the Lord's birth and His resurrection without any understanding of the biblical calendar, many of us are learning to appreciate that God's calendar has been fulfilled and will yet find its perfect fulfillment. We are paying more attention to the cycles of the sun and moon that were placed in the sky not only to provide us light but also to "mark the seasons." We are growing in our appreciation that God has done and will continue to do His work according to His calendar, and we want to learn more about it.

Through it all—through all of our information and misinformation—we abide in the assurance that our salvation rests not in the observance of days but in the finished work of Jesus.

And through it all, we know beyond any doubt that God is working everything for our good if we only love, obey and follow Him.

6

Glory in Suffering

We also glory in our sufferings, because we know that
suffering produces perseverance; perseverance, character;
and character, hope.

Romans 5:3–4

Bob and Sandra were one of our "hippie couples" from the
days of the Jesus Movement. When Sandra became pregnant,
she and her husband began to plan for a home birth, which
translates "without anesthesia." Bob received his training as
Sandra's coach, and they gathered all the necessary supplies
with which to welcome their first child.

When the time arrived and the labor pains began, Sandra
was quite excited and even perhaps a bit smug that they had
opted for natural childbirth.

But Sandra had never before had this experience. As the
pains increased in both frequency and severity, the process was
punctuated with vigorous outbursts of alarm.

"I'm dying!" she shouted to Bob. "Do something! Help me!"
And when she thought she could bear no more, she screamed,

"Don't ever ask me to do this again! I will never have another child!"

As she gasped out those last words, the baby crowned and burst forth into the world. Sandra breathed a huge sigh, looked at her newborn child, then over at Bob. Smiling a bit sheepishly, she confessed, "Oh . . . I might."

Sandra had experienced what Yeshua described in John 16:21: "A woman giving birth to a child has pain because her time has come; but when her baby is born she forgets the anguish because of her joy that a child is born into the world." The truth Sandra gleaned from her own birthing experience contains the message that is needed for our generation. In fact, that word *thlipsis* translated "anguish" is the same Greek word often translated "tribulation." When her baby is born, she forgets the *thlipsis*/tribulation because of her joy.

During their first mission journey, Paul and Barnabas told the new believers, "We must through much tribulation enter into the kingdom of God" (Acts 14:22 KJV).

The Roman Jesus-followers were encouraged not only to "rejoice in hope of the glory of God" but to "glory in tribulations also, knowing that tribulation worketh patience; and patience, experience; and experience, hope" (Romans 5:2–4 KJV). Or as the NIV translates it: "Glory in our sufferings."

Glory in suffering? Rejoice in tribulations? Yes, because, by faith, we see the outcome of our faith.

I call this God's character development plan. "Suffering produces . . . character" (Romans 5:3–4).

God's Character Development Plan

Here in the West, in our attempt to bring more of the unsaved to Jesus, we often do them a disservice by giving them the impression that life will be much easier once they commit their lives to following the Lord. Scripture paints a different picture. Though we have a secure and magnificent future, the path into that future is not always one of ease. Every biblical hero from Genesis to Revelation demonstrates this truth.

Consider, for example, Joseph, who had all those dreams in his youth. In one dream, the wheat sheaves of his brothers bowed to him in the field. In another, the sun, moon and eleven stars gave him homage. Nice future, if indeed his dreams were to become reality, but the path to that destiny came with much heartache/persecution/tribulation.

The brothers were enraged with his favorite-son status and his royal, multicolored robe. The first chance they got, they sold him into slavery to a group of Midianite travelers on their way to Egypt, dipped his coat in animal blood and pretended he had been killed by a wild beast.

Character formation!

Although he rose quickly in the estimation of his Egyptian master and was put in charge of everything in the master's household, this caused even more trouble. The attractive young man caught the attention of his master's wife, and she tried to lure him into her adulterous arms. Joseph resisted, but her false accusations landed him in prison for over two years.

Perseverance!

The warden trusted him and gave him authority over the other prisoners. Joseph interpreted dreams for two of his fellow inmates, one of whom promised to remember him when he was restored to his position as cupbearer to the pharaoh, but then promptly forgot all about Joseph.

More character building! Shaping him for his future next to the pharaoh.

Joseph passed the test and soon became the most powerful man in Egypt, second only to the king. Only when his brothers made a trip to Egypt to get food during the famine and bowed before him did Joseph "remember his dreams" (Genesis 42:9).

By this time his character was so well formed that he was able to say to his brothers,

> "I am your brother Joseph, the one you sold into Egypt! And now, do not be distressed and do not be angry with yourselves for selling me here, because it was to save lives that God sent me ahead of you. . . . So then, it was not you who sent me here, but God."
>
> Genesis 45:4–5, 8

All those years God was weaving His will into Joseph's life—forming him into a person who could govern a nation with wisdom and insight. When the first martyr, Stephen, was reciting the history of Israel, he said that God rescued Joseph "from all his troubles [*thlipsis*—tribulations]" but struck Egypt with famine, "bringing great suffering [*thlipsis*—tribulation]" upon their land (Acts 7:10–11).

Similar accounts could be given of Abraham, Jacob, Moses, David, Esther, Ruth and many others who endured immense suffering before entering into their destinies.

Paul's observation of the lives of these former heroes of faith plus his own life experiences were the background of those words to the Romans.

> Therefore, since we have been justified through faith, we have peace . . . we have gained access . . . into this grace. . . . And we boast in the hope of the glory of God. Not only so, but we also glory in our sufferings, because we know that *suffering produces . . . character.*
>
> Romans 5:1–4, emphasis added

Suffering produces character. There is no other way.

Delighting in Difficulties

Another biblical scribe admonishes us in this way:

> Endure hardship as discipline. . . . No discipline seems pleasant at the time, but painful. Later on, however, it produces a harvest of righteousness and peace for those who have been trained by it. . . . God disciplines us for our good, in order that we may share in his holiness. . . . See to it that no one falls short of the grace of God and that no bitter root grows up to cause trouble and defile many.
>
> Hebrews 12:7, 11, 10, 15

A harvest of righteousness, peace, holiness and godly character, or a life of bitterness, trouble and defilement—the choice is ours; the suffering, the "tribulation," will come into every life.

Paul got this message so ingrained within him that he could say to the Corinthians: "I delight in . . . insults, in hardships, in persecutions, in difficulties" (2 Corinthians 12:10).

Delight in insults?

Why? Because it afforded him an opportunity to be like Jesus—to forgive, love and bless.

History is replete with testimonies of persecutors who observed believers during their persecution and became radical followers of Jesus. Saul of Tarsus is a prime example.

One of our students from the former Soviet Union told how she had been locked in her room and beaten by relatives when she acknowledged her faith in Jesus. Now, years later, almost all of those relatives are followers of the Way they once so despised.

Tribulation Training

Corrie ten Boom was the only member of her family to survive the horrors of the Nazi concentration camps, including the infamous Ravensbruck. She saw firsthand that the people of God in Europe were unprepared to go through the difficult times that lay ahead of them during the Nazi reign of terror. The rest of her life was spent imploring people to accept Jesus but also warning them that perilous times were ahead. "We are in training for the tribulation," she wrote in a letter dated 1974. "There are some among us teaching there will be no tribulation, that the Christians will be able to escape all this. These are the false teachers that Jesus was warning us to expect in the latter days. Most of them have little knowledge of what is already going on across the world. I have been in countries where the saints are already suffering terrible persecution.

"In China, the Christians were told, 'Don't worry, before the tribulation comes you will be translated—raptured.' Then came a terrible persecution. Millions of Christians were tortured to death.

"Later I heard a bishop from China say, sadly, 'We have failed. We should have made the people strong for persecution, rather than telling them Jesus would come first. Tell the people how to be strong in times of persecution, how to stand when the tribulation comes—to stand and not faint.'"[1]

Corrie became so distraught over the effect of pre-Tribulation teaching that she saw it as one of the things against which Jesus warned, a false teaching that would deceive many. Corrie saw herself as having a "divine mandate" to encourage people to be strong in Jesus in times of persecution.

I, too, have become convinced that the pre-Tribulation teaching—that we believers will be caught up into heaven before the last great wave of persecution and tribulation—is a very dangerous teaching. Although it might seem to be an encouragement to people, it can actually serve as deceit. This teaching would be meaningless to today's persecuted Church—those who are suffering imprisonment, torture and death because of their faith.

Trials, Troubles and Tribulation

As I pondered all of this, I began to do a very simple Scripture study. I recommend this for everyone. I looked up the Greek word *thlipsis* that is sometimes translated "tribulation" in our English Bibles.[2] Interestingly, I found the word rendered by a variety of English words: "affliction(s), afflicted, anguish, burdened, persecution, persecuted, trouble(s), troubled, hardship, sufferings, distress, hard-pressed, harassed, trial(s)."

I began to read through the apostolic writings, using the word *tribulation* every time the Greek word *thlipsis* appears. I found Jesus and the apostles talking about the normal "tribulation" of life, times of "great tribulation" for believers through the centuries, as well as the final "Great Tribulation" that will engulf the whole world shortly before Jesus' return.

In not a single instance did Jesus or the apostles assure us that we will be spared *thlipsis*/tribulation. On the contrary, Scripture after Scripture warns us to be prepared for tribulation, for great tribulation and even for the Great Tribulation.

In Jesus' parable of the sower and the soils in Matthew 13:3–9, 18–23 and its parallel passage in Mark 4:3–8, 13–20, He described the seed (the Word) that falls on hard ground. It springs up immediately, but when *thlipsis*/tribulation or persecution comes because of the Word, the believer quickly falls away. This is normal tribulation that every believer experiences. Jesus warned us to build our spiritual houses upon solid rock, not upon sand. The same storms batter both houses. The outcome lies not in the magnitude of the storm, but in the quality of the house's foundation (see Matthew 7:24–27).

In one of Jesus' last recorded conversations, He answered questions about the time of the end. Reaching back into words from the prophet Daniel, Jesus responded, "For then shall be great tribulation [*thlipsis*], such as was not since the beginning of the world to this time, no, nor ever shall be" (Matthew 24:21

KJV, emphases added; see also Daniel 12:1). Or, as the NIV states it: "There will be great distress [*thlipsis*], unequaled from the beginning of the world until now—and never to be equaled again." This is the final Great Tribulation, the Great Distress.

"*Immediately after the tribulation of those days* . . . they shall see the Son of man coming in the clouds of heaven with power and great glory. And he shall send his angels with a great sound of a trumpet, and *they shall gather together his elect from the four winds*, from one end of heaven to the other" (Matthew 24:29–31 KJV, emphasis added; see also Mark 13:24–27).

Immediately after. This is very clear language. We are not spared tribulation. If we are still around when He is about to return, we do not get out before the Great Tribulation. In the apostle John's Revelation, he sees a host of white-robed people from every nation, tribe, people and language surrounding the throne of God. "Who are they?" John asked one of the elders, and he is told, "These are they who have *come out of* the great tribulation" (Revelation 7:14, emphasis added).

They have come out of the Great Tribulation. Very specific. These godly people have been in the Great Tribulation and are "coming out." Jesus seemed to have anticipated the theology that would permeate our generation and wanted to make it clear that we have no assurance that we will be spared great trials, not even the last great one.

Forty-three times New Covenant Scripture speaks of tribulation (*thlipsis*), always with the exhortation to stand strong, even to the point of persecution or martyrdom. For each eventuality, the admonition is the same: "Endure."

They Endured to the End

Because of his radical faith Richard Wurmbrand spent fourteen years imprisoned in Communist Romania—great tribulation.

He tells some amazing stories about the strength of those who suffered and often died because of their faith.

A pastor by the name of Florescu was imprisoned and tortured mercilessly. His Communist captors used every imaginable cruelty in their attempt to compel him to betray his fellow believers, but he resisted continually. Finally, they brought before him his fourteen-year-old son and began to whip the boy in front of him, assuring the man that they would continue until he gave them the information they sought.

When the father could stand it no longer, he cried: "Alexander, I must say what they want! I can't bear your beating anymore!"

"Father," the son replied, "don't do me the injustice of having a traitor as a parent. Withstand! If they kill me, I will die with Jesus on my lips."[3] The torturers continued their assault on the boy until he lay lifeless at their feet. He died, praising God.

Though this was not the Great Tribulation, it was *great tribulation.*

Wurmbrand tells another story of a Christian who was sentenced to death but was allowed to see his wife one last time. "You must know that I die loving those who kill me," he told his wife. "They don't know what they do, and my final request of you is to love them, too. Don't hold bitterness in your heart because they kill your beloved one. We will meet in heaven."[4] These words penetrated the heart of the officer in charge of the execution.

Years later Wurmbrand met this former officer, who was imprisoned for accepting the faith for which the earlier brother had been killed. The love of God was more powerful than the weapons of death.

This was great tribulation followed by great joy.

This amazing story also came from the persecuted Church: On one occasion a young Russian army officer came to a Christian minister in Hungary and asked to see him alone. The minister led him to a small conference room and closed the door. On the wall of the conference room hung a cross.

The brash young officer pointed to the cross and said arrogantly to the minister, "You know, that thing is a lie. It's just a piece of trickery you ministers use."

"But, my poor young man, of course, I believe it," the minister responded, smiling. "It is true."

"I won't have you play these tricks on me!" cried the young man as he drew his revolver and held it close to the body of the minister. "This is serious. Don't laugh at me! Unless you admit to me that it is a lie, I'll fire!"

"I cannot admit that, for it is not true. Our Lord is really and truly the Son of God," said the minister.

The young army officer flung his revolver to the floor and embraced the man of God, tears welling in his eyes. "Then it *is* true!" he cried. "It *is* true! I believe so, too, but I could not be sure men would die for this belief until I found it out for myself. Oh, thank you! You have strengthened my faith. Now I can die for Christ. You have shown me how."[5]

This, too, was great tribulation accompanied by amazing joy.

Stand Strong

As in former generations, some of God's saints live miraculous lives while experiencing great anguish. In the words of the writer of Hebrews, they have

> through faith conquered kingdoms, administered justice, and gained what was promised . . . shut the mouths of lions, quenched the fury of the flames, and escaped the edge of the sword. [Their] weakness was turned to strength. [They] became powerful in battle and routed foreign armies. Women received back their dead, raised to life again.
>
> Hebrews 11:33–35

Still others, for reasons known only to God, have been

tortured, refusing to be released so that they might gain an even better resurrection. Some faced jeers and flogging, and even chains and imprisonment. They were put to death by stoning; they were sawed in two; they were killed by the sword . . . destitute, persecuted and mistreated—the world was not worthy of them. They wandered in deserts and mountains, and in caves and in holes in the ground.

Hebrews 11:35–38

A part of me does not look forward to this whole process. Like Sandra in the birthing room, we do not enjoy the prospect of hard times or the intensity of the suffering that may lie ahead. Another part of me wants to get it over with so that we can enter into that excellent God-predicted future. Just as surely as the joy of receiving a newborn baby helps a young mother forget the anguish of childbirth, the joy of the future will overshadow whatever suffering we are called upon to endure.

I want to shine! I want to lead many to righteousness. I am assured that everything will be turned for my good if I will stand strong in Jesus. And I am comforted in believing that when that Great Tribulation comes upon the entire world, its duration will be relatively short.

7

Escape God's Wrath

Since we have now been justified by his blood, how much
more shall we be saved from God's wrath through him!

Romans 5:9

I suspect that the strongest motivation for my childhood conversion to Jesus was to escape hell. The fires of hell were well
described by roving evangelists. Heaven was not particularly
appealing because, at that time, I had never seen a harp or an
angel, and floating on clouds for eternity did little to captivate
my childhood imagination.

God never seemed all that upset with my early reason for
turning to Him. In fact, Jesus often used this motivation Himself
to encourage change. The first words out of the mouth of His
predecessor, John, had to do with God's wrath. When John
saw the corrupt leadership of his day coming out to hear him
preach, he exclaimed, "Who warned you to flee from the coming wrath?" (Matthew 3:7).

There *is* a "coming wrath" of God that will encircle the globe.
Jesus Himself, in that discourse with Nicodemus, informs us

that He came not to pour out God's wrath but to redeem us *from* that wrath (see John 3:17). "Whoever believes in the Son has eternal life, but whoever rejects the Son will not see life, for God's wrath remains on them" (verse 36).

Those who do not come under God's protection remain under God's wrath. This is a very important distinction. Because of Adam's sin in the Garden and because of our own sins, our world moved out from under God's protection to where there is only wrath.

"The wrath of God is being revealed from heaven against all the godlessness and wickedness of people, who suppress the truth by their wickedness," Paul writes (Romans 1:18). We are "by nature deserving of wrath" (Ephesians 2:3). "God's wrath comes on those who are disobedient" (5:6), but "Jesus . . . rescues us from the coming wrath" (1 Thessalonians 1:10).

A few years ago I was asked to speak at a prophetic conference. I was aware that most, if not all, of those planning the conference ascribed to the "pre-Tribulation Rapture" theory—that believers will be taken to heaven before the seven last years of history, Daniel's last "week"; that believers will be raptured before the Tribulation of those days and most assuredly before the earth experiences God's poured-out wrath at the end of the seven years.[1]

A few days before the conference, one of the planners called. "Are you 'pre-Trib'?" I was asked.

"No, I'm not," I replied.

"Pre-wrath?"

"Without question, we never experience God's wrath," I said.

"Okay, that's fine. See you at the conference."

During the meetings I wanted to be sure to hear some of the speakers who espoused the pre-Tribulation theory. I wanted to know where they found Scriptures to support their belief. One of them, a well-known teacher of prophecy, began his message by expressing his belief in this theory, then said, "Now, if this is true, then . . ." and proceeded to give his entire message based upon his presupposition. He offered no scriptural documentation but assumed that everyone believed we would escape the Great Tribulation.

I sat there, wondering how his message might have changed had he begun with different assumptions, and I was left still wondering what Scriptures he had read that made him so confident that we will escape the Tribulation, even the Great Tribulation.

If I am wrong about all this, and Jesus does, indeed, whisk all of us away before the grand finale of suffering upon the whole world, I will gladly go. But even if for no other reason, I would rather be prepared for the worst and be wrong than *not* to prepare and be wrong. I have seen too many people walk away from the Lord because He did not live up to their expectation of a carefree life once they had committed to follow Him.

The ultimate question is whether greater glory comes to God through a lifestyle of surrender that could possibly end in martyrdom, or greater glory comes to Him if we are whisked away before a great time of testing. Why would God allow believers all through the centuries to suffer persecution, beatings, imprisonments and even martyrdom through the vilest of ways, only to release the final generation from being confronted with similar challenges during the Tribulation or even the Great Tribulation?

Maybe I am a total idealist, but if God will give me the energy and the ability to follow Him passionately, and if I could rescue more for Him by staying behind, and if this would give Him glory, then I would like to be one of His volunteers—even if that means martyrdom.

The Wrath to Come

I want to tell you how I came to the conclusion that we are headed for turbulent times, while also walking in assurance that we will escape God's wrath.

Two Greek words—*thumos* and *orge*—are translated as *wrath* in our Bibles.[2] Both are strong words. One, *thumos*, has to do with sudden, violent, passionate outbursts; the other, *orge*, describes an anger that builds up over a long period of time until it finally erupts. Neither is the destiny of a believer.

"God did not appoint us to suffer wrath [*orge*]" (1 Thessalonians 5:9), Paul assures us. We are "saved from God's wrath [*orge*]" (Romans 5:9).

When John has all those visions about the end times, he sees seals being opened and great distress coming upon the earth, but never in those early chapters does he use the word *wrath* to describe what he sees. Only later with the terror of the sixth seal does he mention *wrath*: "[Jesus] broke the sixth seal. . . . The great day of [God's] wrath [*orge*] has come" (Revelation 6:12, 17). This is followed by the blowing of the trumpets after the seventh seal is opened and the bowls of wrath—the plagues—are being poured out. Even then John makes it clear that the wrath of God is not for believers.

"If anyone worships the beast and its image and receives its mark on their forehead or on their hand, they, too, will drink the wine of God's fury [*thumos*], which has been poured full strength into the cup of his wrath [*orge*]" (Revelation 14:9–10).

At the end of the harvest, the wicked are thrown "into the great winepress of God's wrath [*thumos*]" (Revelation 14:19).

The Seven Bowls

Who experiences God's wrath? Those who have the mark of the beast—the unrepentant. Listen carefully to John's description: "Another great and marvelous sign: seven angels with the seven last plagues—last, because with them God's wrath [*thumos*] is completed" (Revelation 15:1). These seven angels are given the instruction: "Go, pour out the seven bowls of God's wrath [*thumos*] on the earth" (Revelation 16:1).

The First Bowl

As the first bowl is poured on the land, "ugly, festering sores broke out on the people who had the mark of the beast and worshiped its image" (Revelation 16:2).

Upon whom? Those who have the mark of the beast. Not on those who have "the seal of God on their foreheads" (Revelation 9:4; see also 7:3; 14:1; and 22:4).

Why would John make this distinction if the believers—those who have the seal of God on their foreheads—were already gone?

Do not forget what happened to Israel! They experienced the first plagues, but then they entered into a time of protection even though God's wrath and judgment were being poured out on Egypt. Goshen became Israel's place of refuge—peace in the midst of God's wrath.

In that earlier scene from John's revelation—of the woman and the dragon—both she and her seed are taken to a place of protection.

The Second Bowl

With the emptying of the second bowl, the sea "turned into blood . . . and every living thing in the sea died" (Revelation 16:3).

The Third Bowl

The "rivers and springs of water . . . became blood" (Revelation 16:4) when the third bowl is released.

The Fourth Bowl

With bowl four, the sun's power intensifies, scorching "people with fire. They were seared by the intense heat and they cursed the name of God, who had control over these plagues, but they refused to repent and glorify him" (Revelation 16:8–9).

No repentance! Only cursing.

The Fifth Bowl

Bowl number five is aimed directly at the "throne of the beast, and its kingdom was plunged into darkness. People gnawed their tongues in agony and cursed the God of heaven because of their pains and their sores, but they refused to repent of what they had done" (Revelation 16:10–11).

Judgment is being meted out appropriately to the Antichrist and his kingdom—those following his evil ways. Still, in spite of intense suffering, there is obstinate rebellion on the part of the lost.

The Sixth Bowl

The Euphrates River dries up when the sixth bowl is released "to prepare the way for the kings from the East" so that "the kings of the whole world" could be gathered together "to the place that in Hebrew is called Armageddon" for "the battle on the great day of God Almighty" (Revelation 16:12, 14, 16).

Armageddon, or *Har-Megiddo* (Mountain of Megiddo), is the site of Israel's ancient battleground where decisive battles were won or lost. It appears that this will also be the place where Satan will muster every weapon in his arsenal, hoping against hope that he can somehow regain the victory he temporarily won in the Garden of Eden but lost in the Garden of Gethsemane. The bowls of wrath apparently serve only to cause Satan and his hosts to dig in their heels even more deeply in their rebellion.

The Seventh Bowl

"The seventh angel poured out his bowl into the air. And a mighty shout came from the throne in the Temple, saying, 'It is finished!'" (Revelation 16:17 NLT).

Believers, protected through the whole process, must breathe a great sigh of relief. The end has arrived.

"Flashes of lightning, rumblings, peals of thunder" are released in heaven, as the earthquake of all earthquakes strikes the earth.

> No earthquake like it has ever occurred since mankind has been on earth, so tremendous was the quake. The great city split into three parts, and the cities of the nations collapsed. . . . Every island fled away and the mountains could not be found. From the sky huge hailstones, each weighing about a hundred pounds, fell on people. And they cursed God on account of the plague of hail, because the plague was so terrible.
>
> Revelation 16:18–21

Zechariah also sees a huge earthquake. Same one? This would seem so, since Zechariah's earthquake is also the precursor to the Lord's descent. In neither Zechariah's earthquake nor John's earthquake is the wrath directed toward believers. "This is the plague with which the LORD will strike all the nations that fought against Jerusalem" (Zechariah 14:12).

Great upheavals but a secure future. The skies are about to open. The earth is being prepared for the return of the King and a reign of peace.

For us? Not to worry. We are secure and protected—even in hard times.

And during that last great upheaval? We may be here, but we are protected . . . just as was Israel in those waning days in Egypt.

He turns everything for our good.

Everything!

8

Watch for the Signs

"You know how to interpret the appearance of the sky,
but you cannot interpret the signs of the times."

Matthew 16:3

"How much longer, Daddy? Are we there yet?"

Every parent who has ever been on a long road trip with children has heard similar questions and may have answered, "Watch for the signs. They will tell us how far we have to go."

Though the signposts relating to Jesus' return may not be as easy to read as the road signs on an interstate, Jesus assured us that there will be signs that point us to His coming. "You know how to interpret the appearance of the sky, but you cannot interpret the signs of the times," Jesus chided Israel's leaders. "You study the Scriptures diligently because you think that in them you have eternal life. These are the very Scriptures that testify about me" (John 5:39). In other words, "If you were paying attention to your prophets, you would recognize Me."

There are signs that have been in existence for generations. These Jesus calls "the beginning of birth pains"—wars between nations and kingdoms, famines and earthquakes (see Matthew 24:6–8). In our day, there are also specific fulfillments of prophecy that herald His coming.

Israel Back in Jerusalem

When Jesus spoke of the future of Jerusalem, He predicted that the Jewish people

> "will fall by the sword and will be taken as prisoners to all the nations. Jerusalem will be trampled on by the Gentiles until the times of the Gentiles are fulfilled. . . . When these things begin to take place . . . your redemption is drawing near. . . . This generation will certainly not pass away until all these things have happened."
>
> Luke 21:24, 28, 32

"Prisoners to all the nations"—an amazingly apt description of the plight of the Jewish people for all the centuries since the fall of Jerusalem in AD 70.

"Trampled on by the Gentiles"—Romans, Byzantines, Muslims, Crusaders, Turks, British.

"Until"—not until 1967 did a sovereign nation of Israel regain possession of their capital city.

"When these things begin to take place . . . your redemption is drawing near." These things have clearly begun.

"This generation will not pass away until all these things have happened." Does this mean that the generation who saw Israel's return to Jerusalem will not die before the end of the age and the return of Jesus? It would seem so.

Though Jesus told His disciples that "no one knows" the day nor the hour of His coming (Matthew 24:36), at the same time He said that His coming would be "as it was in the days of Noah" (verse 37). Noah knew the season of the flood. The ark was prepared and the animals began to come.

Paul tells the Thessalonians that Jesus is not coming to believers like a thief in the night. Only to unbelievers does He make a surprise return (see 1 Thessalonians 5:1–4).

Jewish People Coming to Faith

During that last week of Jesus' life, when He knew that He would soon be executed, He began to give other clues about His return.

On His way up the Mount of Olives one day, He wept as He looked back toward the city. "Jerusalem, Jerusalem! . . . Your house is left to you desolate. For I tell you, you will not see me again until you say, 'Blessed is he who comes in the name of the Lord'" (Matthew 23:37–39).

Clue #1: Jesus will not return until a significant number of Jewish people, even Jewish leaders, are ready to receive Him.

"The Temple will be destroyed, but you will again return to Jerusalem and will be ready to welcome Me before I return" (my paraphrase).

Centuries ago, Bible readers began to believe that the Jewish people would one day return to the land of their inheritance and that they would come to believe in Jesus as their Messiah.

The Geneva Bible, published in 1560, arose out of that believers' movement. Commenting on one of Paul's remarks to the Romans, the Geneva Bible says, "When both they [the Jews] and the Gentiles shall embrace Christ, the world shall be restored to a new life."[1] In other words, "The Jews will one day turn to Jesus."

Eighteenth-century Church of Scotland preacher Thomas Boston was confident, along with many of his peers, that a time would come when Israel would be redeemed. In a sermon preached in 1716, "Encouragement to Pray for the Conversion of the Jews," he said, "The now blinded and rejected Jews shall at length be converted into the faith of Christ, and join themselves to the Christian Church."[2]

We may not like the way Thomas Boston expressed himself; we may not believe that these returning Jewish believers will need to "join themselves to the Christian Church" but rather be gathered in their own synagogues to worship their own Messiah Yeshua/Jesus. We may even wince at the use of the word *convert*, since they are simply acknowledging their own Messiah, but Boston had caught hold of a truth that would only later come to fruition.

Boston also understood, on the basis of Romans 11:12, 15, that the Jewish return would affect world revival. "Are you longing for a revival to the churches, now lying like dry bones," he wrote, "would you fain have the Spirit of life enter into them? Then pray for the Jews. 'For if the casting away of them be the reconciling of the world; what shall the receiving of them be, but life from the dead?'"[3]

This expectation of Israel's return to the land and to the Lord was still thriving in the time of Charles Spurgeon in the nineteenth century. In an 1855 volume of sermons, he wrote, "The day shall come when the Jews . . . shall be gathered in again. Until that shall be, the fullness of the church's glory can never come."[4]

All these from earlier centuries were seeing in the Spirit what we have seen with our own eyes—Israel's return to the Promised Land and Jewish people coming to the Lord in increasing numbers.

The year 1967 was an amazing year for the beginning of this fulfillment. Not only was this the year Israel reclaimed Jerusalem in the Six-Day War, but this was also the beginning of the movement in which tens of thousands of Jewish men and women began to believe that Jesus/Yeshua is indeed the promised Messiah of Israel.

The lead article in the June 21, 1971, issue of *Time* magazine addresses "The Jesus Revolution." Three times the article mentions 1967 as the beginning of what also came to be called the Jesus Movement and was the beginning of the charismatic renewal. Writer Richard Ostling, describing the unusual revival of those former hippies-turned-Jesus freaks, mentions this: "Many Jews have also joined, claiming that they are not quitting, but fulfilling their Judaism."[5]

The Jesus Movement produced most of today's senior leaders in the Messianic movement. This was the movement that captured my own heart for the things of the Spirit and, because of Jewish people who were coming to faith in my own congregation, launched me into a passion for the Lord from which I have never recovered. Through these Jewish believers I became acquainted with the burgeoning Jewish believing movement and into a rereading of the prophets.

Prior to 1967 there were occasional Jewish people who believed in Jesus, but the Jesus Movement was the first revival since the first century that began an avalanche of Jewish people coming to faith. This has resulted in several hundred thousand Jewish believers now scattered in churches, in freshly formed Jesus-believing synagogues or house groups, or simply remaining in a traditional synagogue as believers.

This opening of Jewish eyes continues its advance, though not nearly as rapidly as some of us would desire. The Jewish community is also changing its view of Jewish believers. A 2013 Pew Forum survey of American Jewry showed that 34 percent of American Jews now agree that a person can still be Jewish even if he believes that Jesus is the Messiah.[6] This would have been impossible a generation ago.

Jesus pointed to all of this when He said that day on the Mount of Olives, "You will not see Me again until you say, 'Blessed is He that comes in the name of the Lord!'" as if to remind them, "I will not return until you are ready to welcome Me."

This could happen at any time.

Revival Among the Nations

In Jesus' same conversation that day on the Mount of Olives, He told His followers, "This gospel of the kingdom will be preached in the whole world as a testimony to all nations [*ethnos*—ethnic group], and then the end will come" (Matthew 24:14).

Clue #2: "To all nations." Jesus will not return until every ethnic group of the world has learned of Him.

"Every tribe and language and people and nation" (Revelation 5:9; 7:9) must be represented around the throne of God.

Some verses in the book of Romans connect the present world revival in China, Africa, Indonesia, South America and even the Middle East among the Muslims to the return of Jewish people to their land.

> If their transgression means riches for the world, and their loss means riches for the Gentiles [the nations], how much greater riches will their full inclusion bring! . . . If their rejection brought reconciliation to the world, what will their acceptance be but life from the dead?
>
> Romans 11:12, 15

In other words, "Just you wait! When Israel begins to come to know their Messiah, there will be an amazing revival of faith awakened in all the world—greater riches for everyone."

In the late twentieth century, mission agencies around the world caught hold of Jesus' prediction and began a concerted effort to evangelize the unreached people groups of the world. The "AD2000 and Beyond Movement"[7] was formed, targeting those unreached groups. When the task remained unfinished by the turn of the century, other organizations arose.

"Table 71" is "a loose association of Christian organizations committed to working together in partnership among the remaining unreached people groups in the world."[8]

"The Joshua Project" is "a research initiative seeking to highlight the ethnic people groups of the world with the fewest followers of Christ. Accurate, updated ethnic people group information is critical for understanding and completing the Great Commission."[9]

The "call2all" is "a movement of believers from across the globe, working together to see the completion of the Great Commission."[10]

"This Gospel of the Kingdom will be preached in the whole world." We are drawing close.

Nations Against Israel

Zechariah also describes conditions just prior to Jesus' coming: "I will gather all the nations to Jerusalem to fight against it. . . . Then the LORD will go out and fight against those nations. . . . On that day his feet will stand on the Mount of Olives" (Zechariah 14:2–4).

Clue #3: All the nations will gather to fight against Jerusalem.

"The city will be captured, the houses ransacked, and the women raped" (Zechariah 14:2). This is not a pleasant depiction of the conditions prior to Jesus' return. The only way I can read this with any degree of hope is to remember that in those last days of Israel's stay in Egypt, as conditions worsened, those who were obedient to God were protected from the horror.

Clue #4: The city of Jerusalem will be divided.

"Half of the city will go into exile, but the rest of the people will not be taken from the city" (Zechariah 14:2). Not God's ultimate plan, but this has been the recommendation of the United Nations for decades. Give half the city to Israel's worst enemies, enemies who have yet to acknowledge Israel's right to exist and who still consider the nation of Israel to be "occupied territory."

A November 25, 2013, web-based report from UN Watch, states that

> the U.N. General Assembly in 2013 adopted a total of 21 reso-
> lutions singling out Israel for criticism—and 4 resolutions on
> the rest of the world combined . . . : one on Syria, a regime
> that has murdered 120,000 of its own people, and one each
> on Iran, North Korea and Myanmar. There were zero UNGA
> resolutions on gross and systematic abuses committed by China,
> Cuba, Egypt, Pakistan, Russia, Saudi Arabia, Sri Lanka, Sudan,
> Zimbabwe, nor on many other major perpetrators of grave
> violations of human rights.[11]

To perceive the leadership of all the nations turning against the nation of Israel is no longer difficult to imagine. Zechariah's picture may be near, but I am encouraged to believe that this end time attack will be of short duration.

"The LORD my God will come, and all the holy ones with him" (Zechariah 14:5). The ensuing earthquake will open up the Eastern Gate (see Ezekiel 44:1), water will flow out from Jerusalem, down to the Dead Sea (see Ezekiel 47) and "the LORD will be king over the whole earth" (Zechariah 14:9).

Many of these signs could happen very soon. But as we look more carefully at the road signs, we are forced to pause—like pulling over to a roadside park to study the map—and must finally admit that some of the roads on our path are not clearly marked. Or perhaps we simply do not have the expertise with which to read them.

Zechariah 12 also predicts a war that may or may not be the same war described in Zechariah 14. In the earlier depic-tion, "all the nations are gathered against" Jerusalem, but the prophet seems to indicate that Israel will be victorious in that battle.

This statement rings of a great national victory, but there is no mention of the Lord's army visibly entering the battle.

"I will pour out on the house of David and the inhabitants of Jerusalem a spirit of grace and supplication," [Zechariah continues]. "They will look on me, the one they have pierced, and they will mourn for him as one mourns for an only child, and grieve bitterly for him as one grieves for a firstborn son. . . . On that day a fountain will be opened to the house of David and the inhabitants of Jerusalem, to cleanse them from sin and impurity."

Zechariah 12:10; 13:1

Israel will *see* Jesus. They will grieve when they realize that they have rejected their Messiah, but their grief will soon turn to joy as they experience cleansing from sin and impurity.

Is this a *seeing* with natural eyes, or is this a vision of Jesus, much like my friend Eitan Shishkoff had that day in the mountains of New Mexico when he *saw* Jesus on the cross, his Lord's blazing gaze piercing Eitan's soul? We are not likely to know until it happens.

Gog and Magog

Where do Ezekiel 38 and 39 fit into this picture?

"In future years" . . . "after many days," an invading army is to come against Israel. The enemies are Gog and Magog, nations from "the far north," and include Persia (Iran), Cush (Ethiopia and/or Egypt), Put (Libya), parts of Assyria and others. These nations invade "a land that has recovered from war . . . had long been desolate . . . and now all of them live in safety" (Ezekiel 38:8, 15).

Recovered from war and living in safety? This is not a description of today's Israel. Threats of war abound daily with rockets from Gaza or Lebanon and suicide-bombing terrorists lurking in every city. The war Ezekiel describes, like the one in

Zechariah 12, is one in which Israel is remarkably victorious. God intervenes with exacting judgment.

"I will summon a sword against Gog on all my mountains, declares the Sovereign LORD. . . . I will execute judgment on him with plague and bloodshed. I will pour down torrents of rain, hailstones and burning sulfur on him and on his troops and on the many nations with him. . . . I will make myself known in the sight of many nations."

Ezekiel 38:21–23

The victory is so decisive that "for seven months the Israelites will be burying [the dead] in order to cleanse the land" (Ezekiel 39:12), and for seven years, enemy weapons will supply fuel for the nation (see Ezekiel 39:9).

What about John's depiction of Gog and Magog? The Gog-Magog battle he describes follows the millennial reign of Jesus. "*When the thousand years are over*, Satan will be released from his prison and will go out to deceive the nations in the four corners of the earth—Gog and Magog—and to gather them for battle" (Revelation 20:7–8, emphasis added).

Is John's battle the same as Ezekiel's battle? Is Ezekiel's battle also at the end of the Millennium? He, too, spoke of "burning sulfur" being poured on the enemy and his troops.

Using enemy weapons as fuel for the nation does not sound like the way Jesus would begin His millennial reign of peace. Nor does burying the dead for seven months speak of a joyful celebration of His new government.

Are there two battles that engage Gog and Magog in a double-prophecy fulfillment? Until the prophecies take place, we will not have a clear picture. As Paul told the Corinthian believers, "We see only a reflection as in a mirror; then we shall see face to face" (1 Corinthians 13:12).

We have many questions and few answers.

Rise of the Antichrist

Clue #5. One thing is certain. An Antichrist figure will dominate the world stage as we approach the end.

In Paul's second letter to the Thessalonians, he told the believers,

> That day [Jesus' return] will not come until the rebellion occurs and the man of lawlessness is revealed, the man doomed to destruction. He will oppose and will exalt himself over everything that is called God or is worshiped, so that he sets himself up in God's temple, proclaiming himself to be God.
>
> 2 Thessalonians 2:3–4

This language cannot be disputed—the Antichrist in a reconstructed Temple, presenting himself as God.

This anti-Messiah figure is the same man Daniel saw, one who will "speak against the Most High" (Daniel 7:25), "consider himself superior . . . and take his stand against the Prince of princes" (Daniel 8:25) and "exalt and magnify himself above every god and will say unheard-of things against the God of gods" (Daniel 11:36).

This is the beast from the sea in John's Revelation, who "opened its mouth to blaspheme God, and to slander his name and his dwelling place and those who live in heaven" (Revelation 13:6)—the one who will reign over the earth for three and a half years, the latter half of Daniel's "week."

This future world leader will be Satan's personal representative in his final attempt to lead all of Adam's family astray and to prevent the return of King Jesus.

Those Last Seven Years

Daniel's vision contains a number of predictions about "the time of the end" (Daniel 12:4, 9, see also verse 13)—specific prophecies about the coming of "Messiah" (Daniel 9:25 KJV), and a future world ruler "waging war against the holy people and defeating them" (Daniel 7:21). This evil prince will "destroy the city and the sanctuary . . . [and] will confirm a covenant with many for one 'seven.' In the middle of the 'seven' he will . . . set up an abomination that causes desolation, until the end that is decreed is poured out on him" (Daniel 9:26–27). In the same context, Daniel is told, "The end will come like a flood" (verse 26).

A seven-year covenant with something changing in the middle of the seven years—thus, two three-and-one-half-year time spans. The angel Gabriel describes this "distant future" to Daniel when

> "a fierce-looking king, a master of intrigue, will arise. He will become very strong, but not by his own power. He will cause astounding devastation and will succeed in whatever he does. He will destroy those who are mighty, the holy people. He will cause deceit to prosper, and he will consider himself superior. . . . He will destroy many and take his stand against the Prince of princes. . . . Seal up the vision, for it concerns the distant future."
>
> Daniel 8:23–26

Daniel's last seven years seem to include both the latter three and a half years of the Great Tribulation, plus the emptying of the bowls of wrath just prior to the end—a time when, if believers are still here on earth, they will be shielded from God's wrath.

Daniel's prophecy is quite clear about the earlier three-and-a-half-year prediction when "the holy people will be delivered into his hands [the evil ruler] for a time, times and half a time" (Daniel 7:25). John mentions the same length of time, called "forty-two months," when this world dictator will be "given power to wage war against God's holy people and to conquer them" (Revelation 13:5, 7).

There are many signs along this road. Some are clearly visible; some are difficult to read. Some have happened; some seem to be some distance away.

Several years ago I was pondering this whole end time scenario. Scripture says that "his bride has made herself ready" (Revelation 19:7), but I knew that the Church has not yet made herself ready. She is not living in the unity for which Jesus prayed. She is not living in the purity or the power He promised.

About that time I had an evening wedding. I happened to be in the church building during the afternoon when the bride came over to look at the sanctuary and make sure that everything was in order. When I saw her I was shocked. She did not look very much like a bride. Her hair was not well coiffed, and she was wearing a rather unattractive casual outfit.

A few hours later I stood at the front of that sanctuary and saw that same bride ready for her groom. *What a transformation in such a short period of time!* I mused. She was immaculately groomed in an indescribably beautiful wedding gown.

I smiled to myself as the Lord nudged me and said, *See there! I can pull things together rather rapidly.*

The signs may not always be easy to read, but we must remember two things: We are victorious through it all, and we are more powerful than any force that can come against us. The darkest days are our brightest hours.

9

Do Not Be Deceived

"Watch out that no one deceives you."

Matthew 24:4

My feelings as a Christian point me to my Lord and Savior as a fighter. . . . In boundless love as a Christian and as a man I read through the passage which tells us how the Lord at last rose in His might and seized the scourge to drive out of the Temple the brood of vipers and adders. . . . As a Christian I have also a duty to my own people. . . . The Party, as such, stands for positive Christianity, but does not bind itself in the matter of creed to any particular confession.[1]

These are the words of Adolf Hitler, given during the early development of his National Socialist Party in the early 1920s.

"Positive Christianity"!

Hitler's deceptive words caught the Church off guard. More than ninety percent of the German people were baptized and confirmed "Christians." Thousands of leaders bought in to Hitler's idea of "positive Christianity," a Christianity that expelled

Jews from the Church, even Jews who had risen in leadership within the Church—all under the guise of keeping the races pure. In those early days there was no mention of eradicating the Jews, but simply separating them to themselves.

Eric Metaxas's biography of Dietrich Bonhoeffer describes the rationale of those leaders.

> Someplace in the deep and wide abyss betwixt these two existed a strange group who did not think there was an abyss, and who wished to create a seamless connection between National Socialism and Christianity. They saw no theological problem with the project, and during much of the 1930s, they constituted a powerful force in Germany. . . . One German Christian leader, Reinhold Krause, said that Martin Luther had left Germans with "a priceless legacy: the completion of the German Reformation in the Third Reich."[2]

Martin Luther, almost four centuries earlier, had prepared the way for this kind of thinking. Even though in his early years he had encouraged gentleness in dealing with the Jewish people, hoping that this would result in their conversion to Christianity, in his later years he became vehemently anti-Semitic. In those closing years of Luther's life, he became so irate by Jewish refusal to accept Christianity that he

> proposed seven measures of "sharp mercy" that German princes could take against the Jews: (1) burn their schools and synagogues; (2) transfer Jews to community settlements; (3) confiscate all Jewish literature, which was blasphemous; (4) prohibit rabbis to teach, on pain of death; (5) deny Jews safe-conduct, so as to prevent the spread of Judaism; (6) appropriate their wealth and use it to support converts and to prevent the lewd practice of usury; (7) assign Jews to manual labor as a form of penance.[3]

Luther's words became fodder in the hands of Hitler and his "positive Christianity" followers. Many of the pastors honestly believed that under Hitler the opportunities for evangelism would increase, but Bonhoeffer and others knew "that a church that did not stand with the Jews was not the church of Jesus Christ, and to evangelize people into a church that was not the church of Jesus Christ was foolishness and heresy."[4]

In the beginning of Hitler's reign, Bonhoeffer helped form what came to be known as the "Confessing Church," working against the "Nazified official German church." Before his martyrdom, he also led an underground seminary, teaching his students "how to maintain a robust devotional life, praying and studying and meditating on the Scripture daily."[5] Nazism could not seduce those who were spiritually astute.

Let No One Deceive You

Paul cautioned the early believers with these words: "The Spirit clearly says that in later times some will abandon the faith and follow deceiving spirits and things taught by demons" (1 Timothy 4:1). "Watch out that you are not deceived," Jesus Himself warned.

Abandon the faith . . . be deceived by spirits . . . be taught by demons. Watch out!

The seduction that engulfed the German churches was also working among Communist countries of Eastern Europe. "Once the communists came to power, they skillfully used the means of seduction toward the Church," Richard Wurmbrand wrote in his book *Tortured for Christ*.[6]

The Communist government convened a gathering of Christian leaders in the Romanian national parliament building.

There were four thousand priests, pastors, and ministers of all denominations . . . [who] chose Joseph Stalin as honorary president of this congress. At the same time he was president of the World Movement of the Godless and a mass murderer of

Christians. One after another, bishops and pastors arose . . . and declared that communism and Christianity are fundamentally the same and could coexist [assuring] the new government of the loyalty of the church.[7]

One Orthodox bishop had the "hammer and sickle" emblem stitched onto his clerical robes, asking that he now be called "Comrade Bishop." A Lutheran bishop began to teach in the theological seminary that God had given three revelations through Moses, Jesus and Stalin, each superseding the one before. At times, pastors became officers in the secret police, working to silence those who remained true to their faith, often assigning them to years of imprisonment and even death.

From Your Own Number

Paul also told the Ephesian elders, "After I leave, savage wolves will come in among you and will not spare the flock" (Acts 20:29).

The power of deception: "From your own number" (verse 30).

Traditional Christianity will not shield us from deception. Being members of a church will not suffice. Quoting or referencing Scripture may even add to the confusion since the devil himself is quite adept at citing Scripture out of context. Like Jesus, we must be ready to reply, "It is written" (see Luke 4:1–13).

We must know Jesus. His Word must be in our hearts and in our minds. Those who walk intimately with Jesus will be kept from deception.

While some who teach deceptive doctrine may come from among us, they will only foreshadow the coming of the last great deceiver. Both Stalin and Hitler were precursors of that one, yet neither of these is credited with the kind of power that will accompany the great deceiver.

In the meantime, "false messiahs and false prophets will appear and perform signs and wonders to deceive, if possible, even the elect" (Mark 13:22).

Counterfeit signs and wonders.

Strong warning.

Beware Small Compromises

The evils of Communism and Nazism seem evident to us in retrospect. But deception comes gradually. Compromise seems so easy, even safe in the beginning. Yet it ultimately takes us down the slippery slope of destruction.

Often the enemy's trickery comes in subtle ways, directed toward us as individuals. A small compromise can propel one down a path of disbelief and apostasy.

Years ago I had an encounter following a Wednesday evening Bible class. A man, probably in his mid-forties, approached me and asked if we could speak privately for a few minutes. We drew aside, and he began to tell me about his life. He had lost faith in God, he informed me. He had once been a missionary in a foreign country. While in that country, he had had an affair that changed the course of his life. Although he had earlier experienced the power of the Holy Spirit, he had not been willing to teach about that power. His supporting church back home did not agree with his theology, and he knew that he would have lost financial support if he preached his newfound convictions.

As he spoke I remembered words from Paul to the Colossians, that our actions may often affect our faith. "Once you were alienated from God and were enemies in your minds because of your evil behavior" (Colossians 1:21).

Alienated because of your evil behavior, I mused.

"When did you have the affair?" I asked my new friend. "Before or after you compromised your convictions regarding the work of the Spirit?"

"After," he replied.

"That's the reason you had the affair," I said. "And when did you lose your faith . . . before or after the affair?"

"After."

"That explains your loss of faith."

Deception had crept gradually into this man's life.

Another of my friends says, "Sin always takes us further than we intended to go; we pay more than we intended to pay; and we stay longer than we intended to stay."

Question God's Word?

Some of the Church has already crossed over the threshold of deception.

Maybe Jesus did not bodily arise from the dead. Perhaps this Book is not the infallible Word of God. . . .

But Paul said, "If Christ has not been raised, our preaching is useless and so is your faith. . . . If Christ has not been raised, your faith is futile; you are still in your sins" (1 Corinthians 15:14, 17).

And the words of Scripture? "All Scripture is God-breathed" (2 Timothy 3:16).

Evidence for Jesus' life and even for His resurrection is overwhelming for one who is a serious seeker of truth. Lee Strobel, atheist-turned-believer, confessed as much in his book *The Case for Christ*.[8] C. S. Lewis, from a former generation, reached the same conclusion, as have many others. In my own search for truth, I decided that if God indeed had raised Jesus from the dead—and I became convinced that He had—then He must have also preserved the words of the prophets and apostles that will lead us faithfully into His truth.

No Fire and Brimstone?

A casual acceptance of the Bible allows us to reinterpret some critical concepts. Among them is this topic:

"Is there a hell?"

"No," some are saying. "The Lord is too merciful to send anyone to a place of eternal fire. This is not meant to be taken literally. Love ultimately wins, and all will eventually go to heaven."

Yale University philosophy professor Keith DeRose, in an online article entitled "Universalism and the Bible: The Really Good News," states,

> I should be clear at the outset about what I'll mean—and won't mean—by "universalism." As I'll use it, "universalism" refers to the position that eventually all human beings will be saved and will enjoy everlasting life with Christ. This is compatible with the view that God will punish many people after death, and many universalists [do] accept that there will be divine retribution. . . . What universalism does commit one to is that such punishment won't last forever.[9]

But what does Jesus say?

"Then he will say to those on his left, 'Depart from me, you who are cursed, into the eternal fire prepared for the devil and his angels.' . . . Then they will go away to eternal punishment" (Matthew 25:41, 46).

Look up the word *eternal* in any dictionary, and you will find its meaning to be "without beginning or end, lasting forever, always existing, perpetual, ceaseless, endless."

Pretty convincing evidence for a literal hell, wouldn't you say? If Jesus chooses to fulfill His words figuratively rather than literally, I will rejoice, but His words are obviously intended to keep us from the worst place we can imagine, a place described as "fire, hell, eternal punishment, outer darkness."

I choose not to ignore the warnings. I choose to let God's Word be my guide.

Quench the Spirit?

Actively debated in some Christian circles is the work of the Holy Spirit. Are spiritual gifts still valid for today? Does God still do the same kinds of miracles that are recorded in Scripture? Does the Holy Spirit speak to us? What about people who claim to have seen angels or who have had visions or dreams that are interpreted as coming from God?

John MacArthur rattled the charismatic world in the year 2013 when he released his book entitled *Strange Fire: The Danger of Offending the Holy Spirit with Counterfeit Worship*. In the introduction John speaks of "supposed manifestations of the Holy Spirit's power," being confident that the Holy Spirit

> is not an electrifying current of ecstatic energy, a mind-numbing babbler of irrational speech, or a cosmic genie who . . . [causes] His people to bark like dogs or laugh like hyenas. He does not knock [people] backward to the ground in an unconscious stupor . . . attributing the works of the devil to the Holy Spirit.[10]

Much of John's book is the true but unfortunate account of the failure of leaders within the charismatic renewal, men and women who have been guilty of adultery, fraud or other godlessness. These are interspersed with claims of healings and other miracles that were later proven to be untrue, perhaps even to have been staged.

But we must never allow the reputation, success or failure of others to alter the truth of what God has spoken in His Word. Nor should this cause us to reject genuine miracles and other manifestations of the Spirit, however strange they may seem. All we have to do is to read the Scripture to see that those who are ardent, Spirit-filled followers of Jesus may sometimes exhibit odd behavior. John the Baptist's bizarre diet of locusts and wild honey and his camel-hair clothing might label him as a fanatic in the minds of many. Ezekiel's lying for 390 days on his left side as a sign of the sins of the house of Israel, then another forty days on his right side as a prophetic wake-up call to the kingdom of Judah (see Ezekiel 4) could easily be dismissed as the vision of a madman, to say nothing of Isaiah's walking around "stripped and barefoot for three years as a sign and portent against Egypt and Cush" (Isaiah 20:3).

My Bible instructs me to "eagerly desire gifts of the Spirit, especially prophecy" (1 Corinthians 14:1), to "live by the Spirit . . . keep in step with the Spirit" in order to produce "the fruit of the Spirit" (Galatians 5:25, 22), just as I am not to "grieve the Holy Spirit of God" (Ephesians 4:30).

Rather than criticizing those who are pressing in to experience more of God's Spirit, and pointing to excesses that may not be one hundred percent pure Spirit, I would prefer to use my energy desiring to be one who asks to be "filled by the Spirit" (Ephesians 5:18), knowing that I have a Father in heaven who will "give the Holy Spirit to those who ask him" (Luke 11:13). I desire to be so filled with the Spirit that "rivers of living water will flow from within [me]" (John 7:38).

A year after John MacArthur's book was published, my friend R. T. Kendall released a book called *Holy Fire: A Balanced Biblical Look at the Holy Spirit's Work in Our Lives*.[11] R. T. agrees that there are gross excesses within the Holy Spirit movement of our day, including the overemphasis on a prosperity gospel that often uses various forms of manipulation to produce wealth for the leaders, even when those who give may themselves be in financial need.

But R. T. also tells his own story of being overcome in the presence of the Holy Spirit at a time when he had no such expectation. He relates his experience of speaking in tongues, which was foreign to his training in the Nazarene Church.

The Word of God is our antidote to deception.

Endorse "Holy" Unions?

Many church leaders in our generation have decided that sexual love between two men or two women can be holy and that such committed relationships and unions should be celebrated and blessed in our churches. They contend that such couples should receive the same privileges of marriage that "one man–one woman" couples have received since the Creation, and that these men or women can be equally ordained in leadership roles in our churches and seminaries.

According to a report in the August 21, 2009, *Star Tribune*, the largest Lutheran church body in the United States, the Evangelical Lutheran Church of America approved the ordination of non-celibate gays to become ordained ministers. The vote passed by a vote of 559 to 451.[12]

On May 8, 2010, the General Assembly of the Presbyterian Church USA, the largest U.S. Presbyterian body, voted similarly by a margin of 372 to 323. The measure required ratification by a majority vote among the 173 Presbyteries before taking effect, an action that transpired on May 10, 2011.[13]

Other churches, organizations and ministries soon followed the same pattern. Well-known scholar Eugene Peterson, who blessed us with *The Message* translation of Scripture, recently surprised many of his constituents by acknowledging: "I know a lot of people who are gay and lesbian and they seem to have as good a spiritual life as I do." When asked if he would perform a same-sex wedding for a gay couple in his church, he replied, "Yes."[14]

This brought an uproar from among Peterson's followers. "LifeWay, America's largest Christian book chain, threatened to ban his books if he didn't affirm a traditional view of marriage." The next day, he retracted his remarks, saying that even though the same-sex couple would be welcome in his church, "out of respect to the congregation, and the larger church body, and the historic biblical Christian view and teaching,"[15] he would not perform a same-sex wedding.

For some of us this answer was less than satisfying. The bold truth of Scripture on this subject does not seem to have been the cause of Peterson's change.

My Bible still reads, "Do not have sexual relations with a man as one does with a woman; that is detestable" (Leviticus 18:22). Eugene Peterson himself translated these verses: "Don't have sex with a man as one does with a woman. That is abhorrent" (MESSAGE).

Paul wrote to the Romans at a time when sexual deviation was rampant in Roman society.

> God gave them over in the sinful desires of their hearts to sexual impurity for the degrading of their bodies with one another. . . . Even their women exchanged natural sexual relations for unnatural ones. In the same way the men also abandoned natural relations with women and were inflamed with lust for one another. Men committed shameful acts with other men, and received in themselves the due penalty for their error.
>
> Romans 1:24, 26–27

Peterson's translation:

> Refusing to know God, they soon didn't know how to be human either—women didn't know how to be women, men didn't

know how to be men. Sexually confused, they abused and defiled one another, women with women, men with men—all lust, no love. And then they paid for it, oh, how they paid for it—emptied of God and love, godless and loveless wretches.

Romans 1:26–27 MESSAGE

Abhorrent or holy? Which do we choose? The Word of God or the word of man?

But what about those who did not choose their orientation and who, even from earliest childhood, have had sexual attractions for the same sex? We love them unconditionally. The biblical commandment never gives permission to hate people. But we also challenge these to choose a lifestyle of obedience to God's way, just as we challenge each other to overcome desires and temptations that are not in accord with the will of God, and to be reshaped into His image.

Those who have forsaken the biblical definition of marriage would profit from reading the testimony of people like Rosaria Champagne Butterfield[16] or Dennis Jernigan.[17] We must be defined by God's definition of who we are, not by what we feel or think.

Kill the Child?

Much of today's church culture accepts the practice of killing children inside their mothers' wombs. If a woman becomes pregnant, whether married or unmarried, and she has no desire to have a child or the pregnancy comes at an inconvenient time, kill the child! Or go to a legal professional who is in the business of aborting life.

You may object that this is not yet a "child" at all; rather, "it" is a "fetus."

But my Book still calls life in a mother's womb a "child"—a "baby."

Rebekah became pregnant, and "the *babies* jostled each other within her" (Genesis 25:22, emphasis added).

"When Elizabeth heard Mary's greeting, the *baby* leaped in her womb" (Luke 1:41, emphasis added). "As soon as the sound of your greeting reached my ears, the *baby in my womb* leaped for joy" (verse 44, emphasis added).

Baby or fetus? Let God decide!

If this seems like strong, even unkind language, remember that Jesus came to redeem all of us from sin. Many who have chosen abortion now live gloriously free lives in Jesus, even rejoicing for the time when they will see their unborn children in the arms of Jesus.

Reject the Jews?

Millions in churches believe that God is finished with Israel and that the blessings intended for Israel and the Jewish people have now been given to the Church. Present-day Israel has nothing to do with prophecy in this belief known as "replacement theology"—pure happenstance, they say. If Jewish people are to come to Jesus, they should leave their Jewishness, become Christians and join our churches.

I have in my files a letter from a pastor who believes that the modern State of Israel has nothing to do with prophecy.

> I received [your literature stating] your firm conviction that the modern State of Israel is a fulfillment of prophecy. The Christian church today is awash in this type of teaching, and you will rarely meet someone as old-fashioned as I who believes it to be false teaching and a corruption of Scripture.

Unfortunately, my friend's opinion is not all that rare. Much of the Church today does not consider today's Israel a fulfillment of prophecy.

But the prophet Isaiah specifically states that a time would come when the Jewish people would return not only from the east—that would have been from Babylon—but also from the south, west and north.

"I will bring your children from the east and gather you from the west. I will say to the north, 'Give them up!' and to the south, 'Do not hold them back.' Bring my sons from afar and my daughters from the ends of the earth" (Isaiah 43:5–6).

From the north—"Give them up!" Russia, from the far north, refused for decades to allow their Jewish people to return to Israel, but that all changed in the late twentieth century when Communism faltered, and more than one million Russian Jews came out of exile, returning to their ancient homeland. As a result the Russian language has become a major second language in Israel.

From the south—"Do not hold them back!" African nations have also been a part of Israel's return. In the 1991 "Operation Solomon," fourteen thousand Ethiopian Jews were flown from Addis Ababa to Israel during a two-day airlift, though many more thousands of Ethiopian Jews remain in refugee camps awaiting their time of return.

Today's Israel clearly fulfills these ancient prophecies.

[God] remembers his covenant forever, the promise he made, for a thousand generations, [David sang,] the covenant he made with Abraham, the oath he swore to Isaac. He confirmed it to Jacob as a decree, to Israel as an everlasting covenant: "To you I will give the land of Canaan as the portion you will inherit."

1 Chronicles 16:15–18

A thousand generations? That is a long time—at least forty thousand years.

"Did God reject his people?" Paul much later inquires. "By no means! . . . Did they stumble so as to fall beyond recovery? Not at all!" (Romans 11:1, 11).

Deception is here and deception is coming, but this is not a time for fear. "The one who is in you is greater" (1 John 4:4). His Spirit is within. Righteousness is maturing. Everything is working for our good.

Those are His promises.

10

Welcome the King!

"Look, he is coming with the clouds."
Revelation 1:7

I had just made a trip to the airport, not to depart on some international flight, as I often do, but because some friends of mine were arriving, and I wanted to welcome them to our city. "Should we get a taxi when we arrive?" they had suggested . . . but that would have been inconceivable. They were our honored guests. My family and I left our home in order to meet them and welcome them.

The apostle John describes the scene surrounding Lazarus's death. When Lazarus became ill, the sisters sent word to Jesus, knowing that He could heal their brother (see John 11:21, 32). Jesus delayed His return to Bethany intentionally because He anticipated the glory that would come to God through Lazarus's resurrection (see John 11:4).

Four days later Martha learned that Jesus was outside the city. She left her home, later joined by Mary, to greet Him and bring Him back with them. Why? Why not wait until Jesus arrived at their home? Unthinkable! They rushed out to meet Jesus because He was their beloved friend, the One who could help them, and they could not wait to see Him!

When Paul was taken prisoner by the Romans and was being brought to Rome for trial, Luke was a part of the group accompanying Paul. He records the reception they were given outside the city: "The brothers and sisters there had heard that we were coming, and they traveled as far as the Forum of Appius and the Three Taverns to meet us" (Acts 28:15).

"Traveled as far as the Forum of Appius and the Three Taverns"? Obviously quite a distance. Why? Why not wait in Rome for Paul to arrive? They would have plenty of time to visit with him. Not a chance! Paul was a highly respected leader, and the brothers wanted to give him a proper reception even though he was being escorted by armed Roman guards.

Why do today's politicians make such a production of receiving heads of state, often including an extensive motorcade to the airport? Why not rather remain in their residences and await the arrival of their honored guests? Unacceptable! Such a breach of etiquette could begin a major world conflict.

Jesus told the story of ten virgins. "At that time," He said, "the kingdom of heaven will be like ten virgins who took their lamps and went out to meet the bridegroom" (Matthew 25:1).

They did not wait for Him (the Bridegroom/Jesus) to come to them. They went out to meet Him.

A Welcoming Party?

It is important that we remember this protocol as we read about Jesus' return to earth and believers going up to meet Him in the sky.

"We believe that God will bring with Jesus those who have fallen asleep. . . . We who are still alive . . . will certainly not precede those who have fallen asleep. . . . We . . . will be caught up together with them in the clouds to meet the Lord in the air" (1 Thessalonians 4:14–15, 17).

Jesus is on His way back when the saints from ages past and those still alive at His coming will rise to meet Him.

Are we to assume that Jesus pauses in midair, gathers the saints together, only to do a round trip back to heaven with those who have joined Him? Not likely. Is it not rather that we are meeting Him in order to bring Him back to reign upon earth for an unprecedented thousand-year time of peace, as both Zechariah (see Zechariah 14:3–9) and John (see Revelation 20:1–6) predict?

According to Paul, believers who die are immediately with the Lord and will accompany Him when He returns (see Philippians 1:23; 1 Thessalonians. 4:14). The writer of Ecclesiastes tells us that the body, made of dust, "returns to the ground it came from, and the spirit returns to God who gave it" (Ecclesiastes 12:7). Paul explains that the saints still living will not "sleep, but . . . will all be changed—in a flash, in the twinkling of an eye, at the last trumpet . . . the dead will be raised imperishable, and we will be changed" (1 Corinthians 15:51–52).

Could it be that the much-anticipated Rapture of the Church is simply proper protocol—a welcoming party for the King? Is it possible that we are with Him in the air only as a welcoming committee for His return?

Is this not like my trip to the airport, like Mary and Martha's leaving their home to meet Jesus, like the brothers in Rome traveling a great distance to greet Paul or like the bridesmaids going to meet the groom? Will it not be our great joy to rise to meet our honored guest—who is no guest at all, but is earth's returning Ruler? We will hear the trumpet, we will respond to the call of the archangel, we will leave homes and graves, receive our resurrection bodies and ascend to welcome the King.

Resurrection Bodies

All of this will remain somewhat a mystery until the full revelation comes. But one thing seems clear. We—both those from past generations who have risen from the dead, as well as those of us who are still alive at His coming—will receive new bodies.

What about this resurrection body? What relationship does the new body have with the one we have used so long on earth? Will we recognize each other? What kind of body will the new one be?

Paul was appreciative of this kind of curiosity. In writing to the believers in Corinth, he posed the same kinds of questions we are asking: "How are the dead raised? With what kind of body will they come?" (1 Corinthians 15:35).

Paul's response was, "How foolish!" In other words, "Don't you know that what you sow does not come to life unless it dies?"

> When you sow, you do not plant the body that will be, but just a seed. . . . God gives it a body as he has determined. . . . So will it be with the resurrection of the dead. The body that is sown is perishable, it is raised imperishable; . . . it is sown in weakness, it is raised in power; it is sown a natural body, it is raised a spiritual body. . . . The first man was of the dust of the earth, the second man is of heaven. . . . Just as we have borne the image of the earthly man, so shall we bear the image of the heavenly man.
>
> 1 Corinthians 15:36–38, 42–44, 47, 49

I have a package of carnation seeds in one of my desk drawers. I keep it there to take to burials. Using Paul's analogy, I like to compare the disintegrating seed (our dead and decaying body) to the beauty and fragrance of the flower when it blooms (the body that will be raised incorruptible). I want people to understand Paul's comparison of the seed to what the seed produces.

No hostess ever decorated her table with a bowl of carnation seeds. But let those seeds die and the blossoms that result will be used to adorn the world's most festive dinner tables.

That is Paul's description of the resurrection body. Somehow the resurrection body that will be raised from our earthly body is as different as the carnation seed and the flower. And yet, that resurrection body is connected to the body that turned to dust so that we will be recognizable.

How do I know that? We have heaven's own example of what a resurrection body will look like.

Heaven's Exhibit A

We need only to consider Jesus, His death and resurrection. Three days after His death, His body was missing from the tomb, so Jesus' resurrection body is, in some way, connected to the one He had used while on the earth. And yet this new body is different. In some cases, even His closest friends did not immediately recognize Him.

That happened on Resurrection morning when He began a conversation with Mary Magdalene. "She turned around and saw Jesus standing there, but she did not realize that it was Jesus" (John 20:14)—not until He called her name.

Later that day the same thing happened to Cleopas and his friend as they were walking on the road to Emmaus. While discussing the events of the recent crucifixion and their dashed hopes that Jesus was the Messiah, they looked up to see Him, but He "appeared in a different form" (Mark 16:12). The three of them walked for some distance together, their conversation centering around the events of the past days, before they realized to whom they were speaking.

Jesus quoted passages from Moses and the prophets, explaining "to them what was said in all the Scriptures concerning himself" (Luke 24:27). Not until He went into the house with them, "took bread, gave thanks, broke it and began to give it to them" (verse 30) were their eyes suddenly opened so that they recognized Him. But just as suddenly, "he disappeared from their sight" (verse 31).

Cleopas and his friend quickly made their way back to Jerusalem to tell the rest of the disciples what had happened. "While they were still talking about this, Jesus himself stood among them and said to them, 'Peace be with you'" (verse 36).

This so frightened the disciples that they thought they were seeing a ghost (see verse 37). And even though Jesus showed them the scars in His hands and feet, they were still not convinced that this was a real live person in front of them. Not until He asked for something to eat, "they gave him a piece of broiled fish, and he took it and ate it in their presence" (verse 42–43), were they sure this was really Jesus in a resurrected body who stood before them.

Jesus' appearance in a room where "the doors [were] locked for fear" (John 20:19) seems to have been repeated several times. Over the next forty days, He appeared and disappeared at will, sometimes to only one or two people. On another occasion He revealed Himself to His disciples on the shore of the Sea of Galilee while they were fishing (see John 21). And at least once, He showed up before a crowd of as many as five hundred (see 1 Corinthians 15:6).

During these appearances, He continually "spoke about the kingdom of God" (Acts 1:3). He told the disciples to stay in Jerusalem until Holy Spirit power came upon them. They would then begin a proclamation that would ultimately reach "to the ends of the earth" (verse 8).

And then one day, when Jesus went out to the Mount of Olives, "to the vicinity of Bethany, he lifted up his hands and blessed them. While he was blessing them, he left them and was taken up into heaven" (Luke 24:50–51).

As the disciples gazed with yearning toward the sky, two angels standing nearby reassured them that He would return to earth "in the same way you have seen him go" (Acts 1:11)—a return that is yet to come.

So, what will we be able to do in our resurrection bodies? We can walk, talk and eat just as we can in our present bodies. We can appear in different forms. We can appear and disappear through closed and locked doors. (I wonder if we will be able to travel at the speed of thought?) We may still carry some of the scars from our old bodies, but I would assume that Jesus' scars served only to glorify the Father and to prove to His friends that He was indeed the same Jesus who had been beaten, crucified and buried. (I rather suspect that our resurrection bodies may not be scarred in any way. But if they are, those scars will also glorify the Lord.)

Our resurrection bodies will be gloriously beautiful. Never forget Paul's description: "sown perishable . . . raised imperishable . . . sown in weakness . . . raised in power . . . sown a natural body . . . raised a spiritual body."

And never forget the difference between the carnation seed and the flower.

King of the Universe

So many centuries ago Zechariah predicted: "The LORD my God will come, and all the holy ones with him. . . . The LORD will be king over the whole earth. On that day there will be one LORD, and his name the only name" (Zechariah 14:5, 9).

Zechariah was seeing the same vision that Paul later described: "The Lord Jesus [will be] revealed from heaven . . . with his powerful angels" (2 Thessalonians 1:7).

Saints and angels—all a part of the King's entourage. Those who have died and those who are still alive. Again, a reminder: "According to the Lord's word . . . we who are still alive, who are left until the coming of the Lord, will certainly not precede those who have fallen asleep," Paul assured the believers in Thessalonica (1 Thessalonians 4:15). At the same time, heaven bursts open with, "Hallelujah! Salvation and glory and power belong to our God. . . . For our Lord God Almighty reigns. Let us rejoice and be glad and give him glory! For the wedding of the Lamb has come, and his bride has made herself ready" (Revelation 19:1, 6–7).

And all the inhabitants of the earth?

Still reeling from the earthquake on the Mount of Olives, they will be watching as the Eastern Gate of the Old City of Jerusalem opens and splits the Muslim cemetery just outside that now-closed gate. This gate, the Beautiful Gate (see Acts 3:2), is the one through which Jesus and His friends so frequently walked on their way to the Mount of Olives and to the home of their friends Mary, Martha and Lazarus in Bethany.

The Eastern Gate Will Open

Centuries before Jesus arrived the first time, Ezekiel prophesied about that Eastern gate.

> The outer gate . . . the one facing east . . . was shut. The LORD said to me, "This gate is to remain shut. It must not be opened; no one may enter through it. It is to remain shut because the LORD, the God of Israel, has entered through it. The prince himself is the only one who may sit inside the gateway. . . . He is to enter . . . and go out the same way."
>
> Ezekiel 44:1–3

Interesting! Why is this Eastern Gate the only gate of the Old City that has been closed for centuries?

The man who ordered it closed was fulfilling the very prophecy he was trying to prevent. In the year 1517, when Suleiman the Magnificent conquered Jerusalem, he rebuilt the city walls but ordered the Eastern Gate sealed, even planting a Muslim cemetery in front of it. Why? No doubt Suleiman had heard about Ezekiel's prophecy and was attempting to thwart any future Messiah's plans to enter through that gate, since no Jewish Messiah would defile himself by walking through a Muslim cemetery.

If Suleiman had read Zechariah's prophecy, he would have known about the earthquake that will happen when the Messiah returns, an earthquake that will rip apart the cemetery and open the gate for Jesus' entrance.

The Dead Sea Will Thrive

Another amazing geographical event occurs on the day when Jesus returns. Both Ezekiel and Zechariah speak of living water that begins to flow from Jerusalem, "out from under the threshold of the temple toward the east" (Ezekiel 47:1). Zechariah sees the water flowing "half of it east to the Dead Sea and half of it west to the Mediterranean Sea" (Zechariah 14:8). Ezekiel says, "The water was coming down from under the south side of the temple, south of the altar," growing deeper and deeper until it ultimately "enters the Dead Sea" (Ezekiel 47:1, 8).

This living water that begins with a trickle from under the Temple—then ankle deep, knee deep, waist deep, and finally "deep enough to swim in—a river that no one could cross" (Ezekiel 47:5)—makes everything fresh. The salt water of the Dead Sea becomes fresh. Fruit trees line the banks on both sides of what has now become a river. "Their leaves will not wither, nor will their fruit fall. Every month they will bear fruit, because the water from the sanctuary flows to them.

Their fruit will serve for food and their leaves for healing"
(Ezekiel 47:12).

Peace Will Prevail

Ezekiel's prophecy seems to have a double fulfillment. The
first is when Jesus returns to reign over a world of peace for
a thousand years (see Revelation 20:1–7). This will be a time
when people live long lives, but death has not yet been defeated
(see Isaiah 65:20). The second, the final destiny of redeemed
mankind, is when we enter into eternity future, and the saved
of Adam's children again have access to the Tree of Life and
live forever (see Genesis 3:22–24; Revelation 22:1–5).

Both Micah and Isaiah foresee a time of world peace when
swords will be beaten into plowshares, and spears into pruning
hooks, since "nation will not take up sword against nation,
nor will they train for war anymore" (Isaiah 2:4; Micah 4:3).
"Everyone will sit under their own vine and under their own
fig tree, and no one will make them afraid" (Micah 4:4).

The world peace of which the prophets speak affects not only
men and nations, swords and pruning hooks—not only a time
when men sit under their own fig trees and enjoy sweet fellowship with God and with each other—but the animal kingdom as
well. Adam's generations, sons and daughters of the one who
named all the animals in the first place (see Genesis 2:19), are
restored to fellowship with the animals and the animals with
each other—the wild and the tame living together in peace.

> The wolf will live with the lamb, the leopard will lie down
> with the goat, the calf and the lion and the yearling together;
> and a little child will lead them. The cow will feed with the
> bear, their young will lie down together, and the lion will eat
> straw like the ox. The infant will play near the cobra's den,
> and the young child will put its hand into the viper's nest. They

will neither harm nor destroy on all my holy mountain, for the earth will be filled with the knowledge of the LORD as the waters cover the sea.

Isaiah 11:6–9

I do not know about you, but I look forward to that day. I have stroked and brushed a horse's mane and ridden bareback across open fields . . . but lions? I keep telling all the children that I will jump on a lion's back, they on the backs of tigers, and we will challenge each other to a race!

I assume also that during the thousand years of Jesus' reign we will be energetic until we are, let's say, six or seven hundred years old. Isaiah says, "As the days of a tree, so will be the days of my people" (Isaiah 65:22). It seems to me that we will be restored to the pre-Flood days when centenarians are considered young since "the one who dies at a hundred will be thought a mere child" (Isaiah 65:20).

This will be a remarkable time. The devil himself has been seized, bound and thrown into the Abyss, which is locked and sealed over him for a thousand years (see Revelation 20:2–3). All the nations will soon learn that, in order to thrive—especially if they want to continue to have rainfall—they will need to send representatives to the Feast of Tabernacles in Jerusalem annually "to worship the King, the LORD Almighty" (Zechariah 14:16).

Do you begin to understand why Paul, contemplating the future when Jesus would return, told the believers at Thessalonica, "Encourage one another with these words" (1 Thessalonians 4:18)?

This is also the reason I can keep believing—and encouraging others to believe—that regardless of how difficult the times may become, there is victory ahead. The King is coming, and He works everything for our good.

11

Recapture Godly Imagination

"Inherit the kingdom prepared for you from the foundation of the world."

Matthew 25:34 NKJV

I smile every time I think about the coming millennial Kingdom and eternity future. We need to pay more attention to the closing chapters of John's Revelation and parallel Scriptures that speak of those times to come. The biblical description of our future is far more than harps and clouds.

I am convinced that, in our desire to close off ungodly imaginations of lust, pride or greed, we have shut down godly imaginations. Yes, "GOD saw that the wickedness of man was great . . . and that every imagination of the thoughts of his heart was only evil continually" (Genesis 6:5 KJV). Yes, because of man's evil propensity for being "vain in their imaginations" (Romans 1:21 KJV), God gave them over to their own ungodliness. Yes, we are encouraged to "[cast] down imaginations, and every high thing that exalteth itself against the knowledge of God" (2 Corinthians 10:5 KJV).

On the other hand, Jesus continually evoked imagination in His descriptions of the "Son of Man coming on the clouds of heaven, with power and great glory" (Matthew 24:30) and through many other vivid depictions of the Father's relationship with us.

Paul specifically encouraged godly imagination when writing to the Ephesians. After pouring out a prayer for power in the Holy Spirit, for supernatural love to be grasped, then challenging them (and all of us) to come into the fullness of Jesus' nature, he ended with this outburst of praise: "To him who is able to do immeasurably *more* than all we ask or *imagine*, according to his power that is at work within us, to him be glory!" (Ephesians 3:20–21, emphasis added).

More than we can *imagine*!

The most effective way to rid ourselves of ungodly imaginations is to fill our minds with godly imaginations. Darkness is not expelled by concentrating on the darkness but by bringing light into the equation.

Reclaim your godly imagination.

Godly Imagination

Imagine a perfect, all-wise king ruling a world at peace. Imagine that the King is Jesus who sits enthroned in Jerusalem, the center of world government, with heads of state and leaders from every nation coming to Jerusalem to honor Him. "A king will reign in righteousness and rulers will rule with justice," Isaiah foresaw (Isaiah 32:1).

> He shall have dominion also from sea to sea. And from the River to the ends of the earth. Those who dwell in the wilderness will

bow before Him. . . . The kings . . . of the isles . . . will offer
gifts. Yes, all kings shall fall down before Him; all nations
shall serve Him.

Psalm 72:8–11 NKJV

There will no longer be a need for United Nations meetings,
where men and women sit around tables conjuring up peace
plans. No more evil dictators. Not even elected officials who,
even with good intentions, seem never able to bring about those
hoped-for changes.

Imagine Jerusalem as the headquarters of this unusual government, when

the mountain of the LORD's temple will be established as the
highest of the mountains; it will be exalted above the hills,
and all nations will stream to it. Many peoples will come and
say, "Come, let us go up to the mountain of the LORD, to the
temple of the God of Jacob. He will teach us his ways, so that
we may walk in his paths."

Isaiah 2:2–3

"This is the place of my throne and the place for the soles of
my feet," God told Ezekiel in speaking of the future Temple.
"This is where I will live among the Israelites forever" (Ezekiel 43:7).

Imagine those "who are still alive, who are left until the
coming of the Lord . . . [being] caught up together with [the
dead in Christ] in the clouds to meet the Lord in the air"
(1 Thessalonians 4:15–17). All this will take place at the time
Jesus returns to become "king over the whole earth" (Zechariah 14:9).

Imagine those who have survived the upheaval that accompanied Jesus' return (see Zechariah 14:1–8) being restored to long lives, as in the days of Noah (remember Isaiah
65:20–22).

Imagine with Me

Imagine Jewish people becoming the most sought-after people group on earth, constantly expressing their allegiance to Yeshua, to Jesus, the returned King whom they now recognize as "Mighty God, Everlasting Father, Prince of Peace" (Isaiah 9:6). "Ten people from all languages and nations will take firm hold of one Jew by the hem of his robe and say, 'Let us go with you, because we have heard that God is with you'" (Zechariah 8:23).

Imagine the synagogues of the world as centers of Jesus-worship.

Imagine a world where holiness is the norm. What the first Adam forfeited in the Garden, the "last Adam," the "second man," restored (1 Corinthians 15:45, 47).

Imagine a world with no oppression and no violence (see Psalm 72:13–14), where "the righteous flourish and prosperity [will] abound till the moon is no more" (verse 7).

Imagine a world of nations with no war machines and no armies (see Isaiah 2:4).

Recapture godly imagination!

Would you mind if I share with you something else that excites my godly imagination even though I know that I could be wrong about it?

One of my Jewish believing brothers in whom I have great trust once told me that he believes the Temple Mount was the geographical location where God created Adam and Eve. A little later one of our tour guides mentioned that a dominant thought among the Jewish rabbis is that the Temple Mount is the place where God took *adamah* (earth) from the area of the Temple Mount and made *Adam* (man).

I was stunned. Even though I trust my brother/friend, I had never known him to teach anything that seemed so absurd. After all, did we not all know that the Garden of Eden was somewhere in the area of the Tigris and Euphrates Rivers? Were these not two of the headwaters whose origin was the river in the Garden?

But the thought kept roaming around in my head.

And then one day as I was pondering the whole idea, I remembered that the "earth was divided" in the days of Peleg (see Genesis 10:25; 1 Chronicles 1:19). Until the days of Peleg, the continents were all in one place and the seas were one body of water (see Genesis 1:9). Obviously, the continents and islands, as we know them today, were not formed until the earth was divided. So perhaps, when there was a great shift in the continents, the present Temple Mount and the area eastward were separated.

When, in the following year, I began my annual reading of the Torah, the first five books of Moses, I had to go no further than Genesis 2 to be stopped, stunned again. "A river watering the garden flowed from Eden; from there it was separated into four headwaters. The name of the first is the Pishon. . . . The name of the second river is the Gihon" (Genesis 2:10–11, 13).

The Gihon? I thought. *Wait a minute. The Gihon is in Jerusalem! The Gihon is where Solomon was crowned king (see 1 Kings 1:33–34). King Hezekiah channeled the water of Gihon into what we now know as "Hezekiah's Tunnel" (see 2 Chronicles 32:30). This whole thing may indeed be true. The Gihon, along with the Tigris, Euphrates and the Pishon, was indeed one of the headwaters that originated in the Garden.*

This begins to make sense, I mused. *God so often ends things where He begins them. Jesus ascended to heaven from the Mount of Olives, and, according to Acts 1 and Zechariah 14, He is going to return to the Mount of Olives.*

If this is true, no wonder Abraham had to go to this mountain to offer Isaac rather than down in Beersheba where he lived. No wonder David had to buy this particular piece of property from Araunah and build an altar there in order to stop the plague that had resulted when he defied the will of God in taking a census of Israel (see 2 Samuel 24).

And why would this not be the place where God wanted the Temple built, the place where He will dwell, and the place to which Jesus will one day return to rule over the whole world?

Could I be wrong in all of this? Of course. But it excites me to think that when we stand on the Temple Mount, not only are we standing in the area where Jesus will build His Temple from which He will rule over all the earth, but we could actually be standing near the exact spot where God created Adam and Eve.

Precursor of Things to Come?

The small town of Almolonga, Guatemala, experienced a foretaste of Jesus' millennial reign a few years ago when the town of twenty thousand inhabitants went through a major transformation. For four hundred years the town had been seen as a "pit of poverty," plagued with demon worship, alcoholism and extreme drought. Four jails were in constant use to maintain some semblance of order.

But a few passionate followers of Jesus accepted the challenge to see the city transformed, moved there and began to preach the Gospel. Person after person responded, and the demon powers were challenged and silenced. By the year 2000, more than 95 percent of the population had turned their lives over to Jesus and the whole area was experiencing renewal. Within a very short time, underground springs opened up and lush gardens were producing vegetables that became the focus of the Department of Agriculture, attracting the attention of believers from around the world. Huge carrots the size of forearms and cabbages of enormous proportions can be seen in a video entitled *Transformations: A Documentary*, produced by the Sentinel Group. Almolonga is now called the "Garden Spot of Guatemala."[1]

Imagine this kind of transformation in every city and every nation of the world.

The Final Battle

Only one hurdle stands between this last great era of world peace and eternity future when Adam's redeemed children are with the Lord forever. As the millennial reign comes to an end, Satan will be released from his thousand-year imprisonment. With all his pent-up fury, he will engage the world in one last attempt to overthrow God's government and establish himself as the supreme world ruler (see Revelation 20:7–8). Satan's forces will go throughout the earth, ultimately surrounding "the camp of God's people, the city he loves" (verse 9) in one final demonic gasp.

His attack is short-lived. God's Word is clear. It is a done deal. Note the past tense: "Fire came down from heaven and devoured them. And the devil . . . was thrown into the lake of burning sulfur . . . [to] be tormented day and night for ever and ever" (verses 9–10).

Judgment of Believers: "Not Guilty"

With the demise of Satan, world attention turns to the judgment scene where all are "judged according to what they had done as recorded in the books" (Revelation 20:12). Believers can stand confidently before the Judge, not because of our own righteous deeds, but because we have accepted Him whose righteousness has been imparted to us on the basis of faith (see Romans 3:20–22). Our adversary has been vanquished, and our Advocate is not only our Defender but the One who has taken the punishment that should have been meted out to us. Ours, therefore, is not a judgment of condemnation but a judgment of assignment for the coming eternal Kingdom.

In one of Jesus' Kingdom parables, a king returning to his domain gives one servant "charge of ten cities," while another is given "charge of five cities" (Luke 19:17, 19). Same eternal blessing, different assignments.

For those who have refused salvation, John sees a horrifying end: "Anyone whose name was not found written in the book of life was thrown into the lake of fire" (Revelation 20:15), a place never intended for Adam's child. Yet this is the destiny of those who have refused salvation (see John 3:17, 36). When Jesus was describing the end times, He said the disobedient are condemned to the "eternal fire prepared [not for mankind but] for the devil and his angels" (Matthew 25:41).

Eternity Future

Following the judgment scene, the ultimate intention for man at the Creation will finally be reached—God and humanity living together, face to face, in total unity for all eternity in "a new heaven and a new earth" (Revelation 21:1). This is not a make-believe earth and heaven, but an earth that is reunited with heaven as in the Garden at the beginning. This new earth still has cities and nations, with kings. We serve and we reign with the Lord on this new and perfect earth forever and ever.

God tells us very little about eternity future but seems to encourage us with wild imagination. In the closing verses of John's Revelation, he sees the New Jerusalem "coming down out of heaven from God" (Revelation 21:2).

A loud voice from the throne is heard.

"Look! God's dwelling place is now among the people, and he will dwell with them. They will be his people and God himself

134

will be with them and be their God. 'He will wipe every tear
from their eyes. There will be no more death' or mourning or
crying or pain, for the old order of things has passed away."

Revelation 21:3–4

Imagine a place with no death, no grief, no pain. No longer
do we simply live long lives as in the pre-Flood era and in the
Millennium, but we live forever in a place of perfection.

The New Jerusalem is no small, ordinary city. It is 1,400
miles (2,200 kilometers) "in length, and as wide and high as it
is long" (Revelation 21:16). By today's measurements the city
itself would cover all the land originally given to Abraham for
his descendants (see Genesis 15:18–21). This city is also as high
as it is long and wide—about two hundred times higher than
our large passenger planes fly.

Why such a height? Are we able to ascend into the heavens as well as walk with both feet on the earth? We can only
imagine. We do know that the city shines "with the glory of
God, and its brilliance . . . like that of a very precious jewel"
(Revelation 21:11).

The New Jerusalem is well connected to its past. The names
of Israel's twelve tribes are inscribed on its twelve gates (see verse
12), with the names of the "twelve apostles of the Lamb" engraved
on foundation stones of finest gems (verses 14, 19–20). Each of the
gates of the city is fashioned from a "single pearl. The great street
of the city . . . of gold, as pure as transparent glass" (verse 21).

"Nothing impure will ever enter . . . nor will anyone who
does what is shameful or deceitful" (verse 27). God Himself
and the Lamb provide both Temple and light (see verses 22–23).

"The river of the water of life, as clear as crystal" (Revelation
22:1) flows from the throne down the middle of the great street
of the city. On each side of the river is the "tree of life, bearing
twelve crops of fruit, yielding its fruit every month. And the
leaves of the tree are for the healing of the nations" (verse 2).

135

Tree of Life! The tree from which Adam and Eve were not allowed to eat has been restored to Adam's children. God's mercy did not allow Adam and Eve, in their fallen state, to "reach out [their hands] and take . . . from the tree of life and eat, and live forever" (Genesis 3:22). Not even during the Millennium will mankind be afforded this opportunity.

In the last recorded Scripture from Jesus' own mouth, He says, "Blessed are those who wash their robes, that they may have the right to the tree of life and may go through the gates into the city" (Revelation 22:14).

God's "servants will serve him," John tells us, and "they will reign for ever and ever" (Revelation 22:3, 5).

How will we serve? Over what will we reign? Much of this is left to our imagination, but Paul assures us that our imagination is not big enough to embrace all that God has in mind for us. Remember what Paul told the Ephesians? "Immeasurably more than all we ask or imagine" (Ephesians 3:20).

"Encourage one another with these words" (1 Thessalonians 4:18), Paul admonished when speaking about our future. But how can we encourage one another if we never ponder what the future holds?

Never forget that although the process of entering into the millennial reign of peace and the ultimate eternity of love, joy and peace may not always be easy, we are promised that He will continue to work all of it for the ultimate good of those who love Him and are His called ones.

Never forget.

12

Read the Book

The word of God is alive and active.

Hebrews 4:12

On Sunday, March 27, 1977, in the deadliest aviation disaster in history, two Boeing 747s collided on an airport runway in the Canary Islands. The planes burst immediately into flames, killing all 248 onboard KLM flight 4805 that had originated in Amsterdam, and 335 of the 396 onboard Pan Am Flight 1736 out of Los Angeles.

One of the 61 survivors of the Pan Am flight was a man named Norman Williams.[1] Norman, along with his fellow travelers, had embarked on what was supposed to have been the vacation of a lifetime—a cruise that was to have begun on the Gran Canaria Island.

On the morning of the disaster, as Norman was about to leave for the airport, his prayer-warring mother began to weep, sensing that Norman could be in danger. She cautioned him to stand firmly on God's promises and protection.

All was well during the flight from Los Angeles to New York, where the Pan Am flight changed crews and picked up additional passengers. The continuation of the journey to the Canary Islands was routine until they neared the islands. At 1:15 that afternoon, a terrorist bomb exploded in the Gran Canaria International Airport terminal, causing all flights to be diverted to the nearby smaller Tenerife airport with only one runway.

Almost four hours later, the captain of the KLM flight, after what he thought was proper instruction from one of the two traffic controllers on duty, proceeded full throttle for takeoff, even though the Pan Am plane was located at the other end of the Tenerife runway. At 5:06 in the afternoon, the two jumbo jets collided.

Flames immediately surrounded Norman Williams. At that exact moment, messages from Scripture began to fill Norman's mind.

"I will never leave you nor forsake you."[2]

"Fear not!"[3]

"I have summoned you by name; you are mine."[4]

"When you pass through the waters, I will be with you; and when you pass through the rivers, they will not sweep over you. When you walk through the fire, you will not be burned; the flames will not set you ablaze."[5]

"I will not be burned!" Norman shouted. "The flames will not set me ablaze, I stand on the Word of God!" he continued. "I stand on the Word of God! I stand on the Word of God!"

At this point in some strange way—which Norman cannot explain to this day—he saw a hole in the ceiling of the cabin above him and was able to make his way to and through the hole. Once outside the burning fuselage, he slid down the wing of the plane and jumped to safety.

Even though the bones in his left foot were shattered from the jump and he spent many days in recovery, neither he nor his clothes were burned or even singed. No other person in his area of the plane lived. Some of the bodies were charred beyond recognition.

Why would words from the Bible be screaming in Norman's ears in his moment of danger? Because he had read the Book! Not just a casual read but a lifetime of devotion. These words had been his food. Verses from the book of Isaiah were among the words that Norman was almost involuntarily shouting. Not necessarily the words that would be going through the mind of a less casual Bible reader.

Unread Bestseller

There is a great dearth of Bible knowledge in our day, even among those who profess to be ardent followers of Jesus. Whole denominations are being deceived into calling "righteous" and "good" what God has called "sinful" and "abominable." Why? Because of a lack of knowing or respecting the revealed Word of God. Seminarians often experience years of training in which they study about God and about the revealed Scripture but may not actually ever read the entire Bible for themselves. According to recent research conducted by LifeWay, only one out of five Americans has read the entire Bible through, even though we as a nation probably possess more copies in our homes than any other nation in the world.[6]

I love the way Isaiah talks about the thoughts and words of God.

> "As the heavens are higher than the earth, so are my ways higher than your ways, and my thoughts than your thoughts. As the rain and the snow come down from heaven, and do not return to it without watering the earth and making it bud and flourish, so that it yields seed for the sower and bread for the eater, so is my word that goes out from my mouth. It will not return to

me empty, but will accomplish what I desire and achieve the purpose for which I sent it."

Isaiah 55:9–11

Rain and snow? His Word is like rain and snow? How?

Rain waters the earth immediately and everything turns nice and green. Snow, on the other hand, is stored on top of the earth, waiting for the sun to melt it so that it can go down into the soil and bring up the new growth in the proper timing.

Our daily absorbing of God's Word is like that. Some of what we read waters us immediately and makes us spiritually fresh, lush and green. But sometimes the words have no immediate effect; they are being stored up, waiting for the sunlight of God's Presence to strike them at just the right time to accomplish His purpose.

Words from Isaiah and Hebrews had been stored up in Norman and were ready to be released by the radiating Presence of God at the moment of the catastrophe. His life was spared, even though he was surrounded by death.

Downloading Scripture

Years ago I downloaded Psalm 139 to my permanent memory internal "hard drive." I like to think of it this way instead of "memorizing Scripture." Memorizing is difficult; downloading may not be any easier, but it has a better ring to it.

One morning recently I decided it was time to resurrect that psalm. It had grown a bit rusty so I went for a walk with it. Keeping carefully to the left side of the road to avoid the rush of early morning traffic, I became lost in God. When I came to the phrase, "You lay your hand upon me" (Psalm 139:5), it was as though I could feel His hand upon my head—anointing me, empowering me, encouraging me, directing me, assuring me.

Tears began to stream from my eyes. All alone. In the traffic. On Graybar Lane near my house.

I began to wonder all over again why we believers do not spend more time meditating on God's Word, chewing on it, digesting it, absorbing it. I yearn for every person I know to have this life-altering experience. This is the way to overcome fear, anxiety, depression. His Word is true. His Word breathes life into us.

What was it the writer of Hebrews said? "The word of God is alive and active. Sharper than any double-edged sword . . . it judges the thoughts and attitudes of the heart" (Hebrews 4:12).

And what did the psalmist say? "I have hidden your word in my heart that I might not sin against you" (Psalm 119:11).

Yes, that is it! His Word hidden—not on a bookshelf, nor even in my hands as I read it—but in my heart. Repeating His Word so much that it becomes a part of me. That is what "memorization" is—repeating a thing so many times that it is now locked inside you.

Live by the Power of the Word

Late in Paul's life, while imprisoned in Rome, he wrote a request to Timothy: "Do your best to come to me quickly . . . [and] when you come, bring . . . my scrolls, especially the parchments" (2 Timothy 4:9, 13). Though death was near (see verse 8), and Paul had much of the Scripture inside him, he still needed the scrolls. He wanted more.

"The words that I speak to you are spirit, and they are life" Jesus told His disciples (John 6:63 NKJV).

"Keep this Book of the Law always on your lips; meditate on it day and night," God admonished Joshua as he was assuming the leadership of the nation of Israel (Joshua 1:8).

As we face the coming world upheavals, only those of us who read the Book and allow the words to permeate our hearts, absorbing them into our being, will be able to avoid deception. No amount of listening to our favorite preacher or television evangelist will assure that we are hearing truth. We need to read the Book for ourselves and then stand on its truth.

Our standing on the Word of God may not be as dramatic as that of Norman Williams, but it is essential that, as we approach the end of the age, we learn to depend upon the absolute validity of "the Book." Norman was spared from the destruction all around him because words from God were continually circulating inside of him. You and I need that, too.

I challenge you to make His Word a part of your daily food. If you need a reading plan in which you never get behind, never get ahead, but which assures you that, over time, you will read the Word through over and over again, then check the one I have used for years. You will find it in Appendix A.

Yes, God works everything for good for those who love Him and are the called ones. Yet there are times when He cannot give us what He would like to give us because we have not prepared ourselves to receive.

Read the Book!

13

Pray the Word

"When you pray . . ."
Matthew 6:5

"You who remind the LORD, take no rest for yourselves; and give Him no rest until He establishes and makes Jerusalem a praise in the earth" (Isaiah 62:6–7 NASB).

Remind the Lord of His plans for the future restoration of the beloved city? Is He forgetful? Obviously not, but He wants us to take a stand on Scripture and not budge until the answers come. James Goll suggests that the Lord is looking to us, as His divine secretaries, to remind Him of His appointments and of His promises.[1]

"No matter how many promises God has made, they are 'Yes' in Christ," Paul told the Corinthian believers. "And so through him the 'Amen' is spoken by us to the glory of God" (2 Corinthians 1:20).

When we say, "Amen," we are actually saying, "Yes, Lord, I agree with that. It is established in Your Word. I believe it. I want that to be so in my life. So be it. Let it be done!"

There are promises God has given that do not come to fruition until we agree with those promises and, by faith, speak them into existence through our "Amen."

This means that we must learn to pray the Word.

Possibility Praying

One verse changed my life several decades ago when I was crying out for greater victory and greater holiness. I was already keenly aware of my need for prayers of repentance. I had used the penitent prayers of David after Nathan confronted him about his sin with Bathsheba. I had etched those prayers onto my internal hard drive and repeatedly sobbed them out before the Lord: "Against you, you only, have I sinned and done what is evil in your sight, so you are right in your verdict and justified when you judge. . . . Cleanse me. . . . Wash me. . . . Create in me a pure heart" (Psalm 51: 4, 7, 10). The prayers were cleansing, but I still had not gained the victory until the Lord showed me my destiny.

Because of childhood trauma (as so many of us have endured in one way or another), my mind was often involuntarily filled with mental debris. I was often tempted to give up hope of ever having a "pure heart" until I discovered a phrase out of Paul's letter to the Romans: "Those God foreknew he also predestined to be conformed to the image of his Son" (Romans 8:29).

I paused, stunned. *Does this say what I think it says? God has a destiny for me—for us? We are predestined to be conformed to the image of His Son?*

Is this possible? Predestined? My destiny is to be like Jesus?

Amen! I shouted in my loudest internal voice. *I, Don, am predestined to be like Jesus.*

My whole outlook on life changed in one Holy Spirit–revelatory moment. I was suddenly on my way to becoming like Jesus. I had accepted God's promise. I had spoken the "Amen."

By participating with God we become partakers "in the divine nature, having escaped the corruption in the world caused by evil desires" (2 Peter 1:4).

Amen! Yes, I am liking this more all the time.

Soon after this discovery, in reading through John's first letter, I found another bit of truth that added weight to my journey: "If we confess our sins, he . . . will . . . purify us from all unrighteousness" (1 John 1:9).

What a deal! I thought. *Amen, Lord, You convict. I confess. You purify.* This was great news since I had tried for years to purify myself so that I could give God a pure self. It does not work that way. He is the One who purifies. My role is to receive His conviction and confess. He does the purifying.

From that day until this I welcome the convicting voice of the Holy Spirit. One of His roles is to "convict the world of sin" (John 16:8 NKJV), Jesus told His friends. Over and over again I have experienced the victory that God gives when I obey, trusting His Word more than the way I feel.

Identificational Repentance

In the waning years of the prophet Daniel's life, he had an experience that illustrates the way God desires us to relate to Scripture.

One day, while Daniel was reading from the Jeremiah scroll, his eyes landed on a prophecy whose time for fulfillment had come (just as we will do when we read His Word): "When seventy years are completed for Babylon, I will come to you and fulfill my good promise to bring you back to this place" (Jeremiah 29:10), Daniel read.

Seventy years, he pondered. *It's been just about seventy years since King Nebuchadnezzar brought me to Babylon. It is time for this word from Jeremiah to be fulfilled. It is time for the captivity to end, time for us to return to Jerusalem.*

So what did Daniel do?

In his own way, he said, "Amen."

He "turned to the Lord God and pleaded with him in prayer and petition, in fasting, and in sackcloth and ashes" (Daniel 9:3).

He participated with God in the fulfillment of what God had spoken through one of His prophets. Daniel took upon himself, in what has come to be known as *identificational repentance and confession,* the sins of his people and cried out to God.

> "We have sinned and done wrong. We have been wicked and have rebelled; we have turned away from your commands and laws. We have not listened to your servants the prophets, who spoke in your name to our kings, our princes and our ancestors, and to all the people of the land."
>
> Daniel 9:5–6

Though Daniel himself had done none of these things, he saw what God desired for his generation, spoke the "Amen" and began to participate with God to bring the fulfillment.

Daniel cried out to God as though he himself had been guilty of the sins of the nation.

> "For your sake, Lord, look with favor on your desolate sanctuary. . . . We do not make requests of you because we are righteous, but because of your great mercy. Lord, listen! Lord, forgive! Lord, hear and act! For your sake, my God, do not delay."
>
> Daniel 9:17–19

Daniel's prayer is a model for us as we carry before the Lord the sins of our own and former generations.

Daniel had learned to "pray the Word."

Imitating Jesus

What better way to pray than to take the very words of Scripture and make them our own? These words stir me toward prayer continually. In reading the gospels I watch Jesus, knowing that His life is my example. I pray into my own life what I am observing in His. After all, it is He who said, "Whoever believes in me will do the works I have been doing" (John 14:12).

Thus I no longer read the gospels simply to find what Jesus said and did; I read them to see my own destiny. I am to become like Him. The same Spirit lives in me who lived in Him.

When I *watch* Jesus as He touches a leper and read that the leper was "immediately . . . cleansed of his leprosy" (Matthew 8:3), I pause, praying for that kind of power to flow through me. He is the One who told me that I will be doing what He did.

When I *see* a woman who has been "crippled by a spirit for eighteen years" (Luke 13:10) healed in one instant, I stop and ask the Lord to bring that kind of touch through me.

If Jesus could pray and see five loaves and two fish multiplied to serve thousands because there was a need (see Mark 6:30–42), why not I who have His Spirit within me?

I am no longer merely reading fascinating Bible stories; I am being challenged to believe for more.

I pray the Word.

Apostolic Praying

The prayers of the apostles have become my prayers. I store them inside me, waiting for a time to release them.

Some years back when I was to officiate at a wedding, I was asked to include in the blessing over the bride and groom the words penned by Paul from a Roman jail. The prayer became so lodged within me that I have brought it out again and again. I have spoken it over others, and I have looked myself in the mirror, appropriating Paul's prayer for myself, changing the pronouns to make this prayer more intimately personal. Here is my version of Ephesians 3:16–20. Feel free to personalize this passage for yourself and others.

> *May You, O God, out of Your glorious riches, strengthen me with power through Your Spirit in my inner being, so that Jesus may dwell in my heart through faith. And may I have power to grasp the fullness of Your love, a love that transcends my understanding so that I may be filled with the measure of Jesus the Messiah. I praise You and thank You that You are able to do far more abundantly than all that I could ever dream, think or imagine because of Your power at work in all of us who believe.*

You get the point: Pray the Word.

Venting with God

Sometimes I am encouraged but also amused at the display of emotion expressed in biblical prayers. I almost laugh out loud every time I read the book of Numbers and come to one of Moses' outbursts, recorded in all its brashness, right there for all the world to see.

Moses had tolerated Israel's continued rebellion and grumbling as long as he could handle it. One day, after he had had all he could take, he went off to be alone with the Lord, and let go: "Why have you brought this trouble on your servant?" he cried. "What have I done to displease you that you put the burden of all these people on me? Did I conceive all these people? Did I give them birth?" he ranted. "Why do you tell me to carry them in my arms, as a nurse carries an infant, to the land you promised on oath to their ancestors?" (Numbers 11:11–12).

He could have added, "I did not want to do this in the first place, remember? You are the One who insisted on my coming. I was perfectly happy in Midian with my wife and boys."

But Moses was not finished. He had a trump up his sleeve: "I cannot carry all these people by myself; the burden is too heavy for me. If this is how you are going to treat me, please go ahead and kill me" (Numbers 11:14–15).

I wonder if Moses waited to see if lightning would strike, but God did not seem overly disturbed by the outburst. This both encourages and challenges me to express every emotion inside me. Why not? He knows each one anyway. Why hold back?

Seemingly ignoring this explosion, the Lord says to Moses: "I'll help you out. Bring Me some of your key leaders and I'll take some of My Spirit I have put on you and put the Spirit on them. They'll help you. And, by the way, they keep begging for meat, so I'll give them meat—for a whole month, until it comes out their nostrils!" (This is my paraphrase. You can read Numbers 11:16–20 to get the recorded version of the conversation.)

Moses had fared quite well so far and was still alive, so he continued with the eruption: "Lord, have You forgotten that there are several million of us—six hundred thousand, just counting the men? How do You propose to bring meat to that many people? If we killed all the flocks and the cattle, there would not be enough! Not even if we could empty the sea!" (my paraphrase of Numbers 11:21–22).

"Just you wait! You'll see," the Lord answered, and Moses went on his way, perhaps still sulking. This is the man to whom the Lord had entrusted the leadership of an entire nation.

At the time there was no hint of a reprimand from the Lord. Only later, when pride got in Moses' way and he acted as though he and God together would have to produce water again, did Moses get the word that he would not be permitted to enter the Land with his people (see Numbers 20:6–12).

Never be afraid to express your feelings to the Lord. He can handle it. Use the Word as your example.

How Long, O Lord?

A few years ago I was away from home when I received some bad news about someone for whom I cared very much. It seemed that this young man had sunk deeply into drug addiction. He had been daily in my prayers, but I was seeing no effect from those prayers. One of my friends called me, and when I expressed my agony of heart, he said, "Try praying Psalm 13. That might work for you."

I opened my Bible to Psalm 13. I had read it before, since I have been reading the Word all my adult life. But this time it was different. It was exactly what I needed. These words became mine as I walked and poured out my lament. (I find that my legs and my brain often engage together.)

> How long, LORD? Will you forget me forever? How long will you hide your face from me? How long must I wrestle with my thoughts and day after day have sorrow in my heart? How long will my enemy triumph over me? Look on me and answer, LORD my God.
>
> Psalm 13:1–3

Pretty brazen way to speak to Almighty God, wouldn't you say? A good paraphrase might be, "Hey, Lord, remember me? Have You been listening? Are You leaving me here high and dry? Hello, up there!"

But then in the last two verses, it is as though the psalmist catches himself and decides he had better change his tune. Remembering God's goodness, he adds, "But I trust in your unfailing love; my heart rejoices in your salvation. I will sing the LORD's praise, for he has been good to me" (Psalm 13:5–6).

Within minutes, I had this psalm transferred to my internal hard drive. For two hours or more I walked the streets of the quiet neighborhood near the guesthouse where I was staying. Over and over again I prayed: "Will you forget me? How long?" And over and over again when I came to the big word *But*, my spirit lifted and I felt a fresh surge of hope.

Did praying that psalm alleviate all my concerns? No, but it put them in perspective and I had the strength to go on . . . and to keep praying until the answer came.

That is it. Keep praying until the answer comes.

One time Daniel prayed 21 days before his answer came (see Daniel 10). The Israelites prayed for hundreds of years before God sent Moses.

"What took You so long?" we often would like to ask, but that is a question that will have to wait. His ways are always beyond our comprehension.

I hope you understand the urgency. I would be happy if you are now so filled with anticipation for your future times with God that you stop reading *this* book and start reading *the* Book. Start talking to the Lord. Tell Him exactly how you feel about your situation.

And remember, no matter what you are going through or will go through in these last days, be encouraged: He will bring the promises to pass and work it all for your good if you will simply keep loving and trusting, and pray the Word.

14

Wrestle with God for the Victory

"I will not let you go unless you bless me."

Genesis 32:26

Our biblical friend Jacob had an unusual wrestling match one night—a story with immense implications for a Western-style Christianity that often has difficulty persevering through adverse circumstances. All of his life Jacob had been both the deceiver and the deceived. But in a crucial moment he would decide whether to seize the promise God had given twenty years earlier or to continue to be known as Jacob the Heel-Grabber, the Deceiver, the Supplanter.

When put to the test, how serious are we about our commitment to Jesus? How well do we know His promises? Do we have the spiritual energy to prevail when difficulties arise? Would we be willing to wrestle, even with God, until the answers come?

God had said to Jacob's grandfather Abraham, "I will make you into a great nation, and I will bless you" (Genesis 12:2).

But Sarah was barren. Besides, she was well past childbearing age. How could the blessing come if she could not bear a child?

In her impatience and lack of faith, Sarah persuaded Abraham to "help God out" by using Sarah's maid as a surrogate mother. God was not pleased with the arrangement, insisting that the heir would come from Sarah's own womb.

At *her* age—now in her late eighties? She laughed at the ridiculous notion.

Finally, at the age of ninety, Sarah gave birth to Isaac, whose name means "Laughter." Perhaps Sarah remembered her response when the Lord told her and Abraham that she was indeed to have a son (see Genesis 18:9–15).

Waiting in the Dark

For some reason the son of Abraham and Sarah's old age, Isaac, was himself forty years old before he married Rebekah (see Genesis 25:20). Rebekah was expected to conceive quickly and give birth to a son who would become the heir to all the promises God had given to Isaac's parents. But Rebekah was barren. For twenty years she waited, hoping, wondering. *Will Isaac choose another wife since I cannot give him an heir? Will I die before God delivers a son through me?*

After years of infertility Rebekah became pregnant. But another concern soon surfaced. Something was not right with the pregnancy. When Rebekah inquired of the Lord about her unusual symptoms, He replied: "Two nations are in your womb, and two peoples from within you will be separated; one people will be stronger than the other, and the older will serve the younger" (Genesis 25:23).

No doubt Rebekah told her husband about this encounter, but Isaac's later actions imply that he was not in agreement with his wife's apparent word from the Lord regarding the younger son.

When the twins were born, the first one to be delivered was red and hairy. They named him "Harry" (*Esau*) and nicknamed him "Red" (*Edom*). His brother followed immediately, holding on to Esau's heel. His parents gave this child the name *Jacob*, meaning "Heel-Grabber," "Deceiver," "Supplanter," a name that defined the next years of his life.

Isaac favored Esau, the outdoorsman. Jacob was "a mama's boy" who often stayed at home with Rebekah. We can only assume that during those times with her Jacob heard, perhaps over and over again, the story of God's revelation while the boys were in the womb. It would, therefore, have been obvious to Jacob that, since Esau was his father's favorite, there would have to be a change of heart if Jacob was ever to receive the double-inheritance blessing of a firstborn son.

Obstacles to Overcome

The fulfillment of God's Word rarely comes without serious roadblocks. Sibling rivalry seems always to have simmered just beneath the surface in the home of Isaac and Rebekah. This rivalry forms the backdrop for two important events that would shape the family history.

The first occurred one day when Esau came home from a hunting expedition, ravenously hungry (see Genesis 25:29–34). Jacob had just prepared a nice stew, but he was not moved by brotherly love and kindness to share. Instead, he saw an opportunity to grab his brother's birthright.

"Quick, let me have some of that red stew!" Esau cried. "I'm famished."

"First sell me your birthright," was Jacob's response. "Swear to me first."

So Esau swore on oath, selling his birthright to his brother. Score Victory #1 for Jacob.

The second incident happened at the end of their father Isaac's life (see Genesis 27:1–45). His eyes had grown dim, his health was failing and he knew that his time was coming to an end. Disregarding the word that Rebekah had received from the Lord, Isaac sent Esau out into the open country to bring back some wild game for a celebratory meal, after which he would give him the blessing of a firstborn son.

Rebekah overheard the conversation and was not about to let this happen. Unable to trust the Lord for the fulfillment of His own promise, Rebekah took things into her own hands in much the same way that Abraham and Sarah had done in a preceding generation. She persuaded Jacob to go along with the ruse, prepared all of Isaac's favorite dishes, dressed Jacob in some of Esau's clothes that smelled of the outdoors, covered his hands and neck with goatskins and sent him to his father.

"I am Esau your firstborn. I have done as you told me," Jacob lied, as he approached his father. "Please sit up and eat some of my game, so that you may give me your blessing."

"How did you find it so quickly, my son?" Isaac asked, suspicious that something was askew.

Jacob responded cautiously, "The Lord your God gave me success."

Isaac was not convinced. "Come near so I can touch you, my son, to know whether you really are my son Esau or not." But as the old man felt the strategically placed goatskins and caught the scent of his older son, though he was still puzzled, he was ready to bless him.

"The voice is the voice of Jacob, but the hands are the hands of Esau," Isaac remarked as he laid his hands on his younger son and imparted the blessing: "May nations serve you and peoples bow down to you. Be lord over your brothers, and may the sons of your mother bow down to you. May those who curse you be cursed and those who bless you be blessed."

Victory #2.

No sooner had the words left Isaac's mouth than Esau returned from the field to find that his brother, for the second time, had robbed him of his heritage. "Isn't he rightly named Jacob? This is the second time he has taken advantage of me: He took my birthright, and now he's taken my blessing," Esau moaned.

The animosity of the two brothers had now reached an intensity that demanded a quick solution. Esau was determined to kill his brother. When Rebekah found out about it, she urged Isaac to send Jacob back to the home of her brother, Laban.

Remember that we are not simply talking about Jacob and Esau. We are talking about our own lives, our God-encounters, the promises of God and whether or not we have the tenacity needed to hold on until the fulfillment comes.

Your Pillar of Remembrance

The flight from Beersheba to Haran was the setting for Jacob's first encounter with the God of Grandfather Abraham and Father Isaac (see Genesis 28:10–22). While lying on the ground under an open sky, Jacob had a dream in which angels were ascending and descending on a stairway between heaven and earth.

Above the stairway stood the Lord Himself, speaking to Jacob.

> "I am the LORD, the God of your father Abraham and the God of Isaac. I will give you and your descendants the land on which you are lying. . . . All peoples on earth will be blessed through you and your offspring. I am with you . . . wherever you go, and I will bring you back to this land. I will not leave you until I have done what I have promised you."
>
> Genesis 28:13–15

If Jacob had ever doubted his mother's pre-birth revelation, there was no longer a place for doubt. The promise to his grandfather, then to his father, had now passed to Jacob. Jacob carried the personalized promise from the Almighty Himself.

Jacob called the place *Bethel*, "House of God." He set up a pillar of remembrance, poured oil on the rock and swore his own commitment to the God of his fathers: "The LORD will be my God." Following in the footsteps of his grandfather, he vowed to set aside a tenth of all his possessions for the Lord (see Genesis 28:21–22; see 14:18–20).

The Jacob Payback

In the midst of supernatural revelation, God-promises and divine direction, life in the natural goes on. We may have to suffer the consequences of earlier sins and failures even at the same time as we are walking toward destiny.

A few days after his amazing dream, Jacob arrived at the well in Haran and met his Uncle Laban's daughter Rachel, who would become his wife. He bargained with Laban for her hand in marriage in exchange for seven years of service, but then experienced the same kind of deceit that Jacob himself had meted out to his own father and brother. Only after the wedding did he become aware of his uncle's scheme to give him Rachel's sister, Leah, in marriage. This required an additional seven years of indentured servitude before his dowry payment for Rachel would be paid in full. For twenty years Jacob served his dishonest father-in-law before he was ready to return to the land promised by the Lord.

"I see that your father's attitude toward me is not what it was before, but the God of my father has been with me. You know that I've worked for your father with all my strength, yet your father has cheated me by changing my wages ten times," he told his wives as they prepared for the journey home (Genesis 31:5–7).

Eleven sons were born to Jacob during his years away from home, but the memory of his last encounter with Esau was still fresh. Jacob sent his wives, children and servants ahead with lavish peace offerings for Esau—hundreds of goats, sheep, camels and other livestock. "Your servant Jacob is coming behind us," they were instructed to say (Genesis 32:20).

With the family sent on before him, Jacob was now alone—alone with himself and his thoughts about his fractured relationship with his brother, who might still want to kill him for his trickery. Alone with the God of that former encounter twenty years earlier, the God of Isaac and Abraham.

Hold On

Under the open skies Jacob met the Lord a second time (see Genesis 32:24–30). A Man began to wrestle with him, but Jacob knew that this was another God-encounter.

"Let me go, for it is daybreak," the Man cried.

"I will not let you go unless you bless me," Jacob responded boldly. Although the Man injured Jacob's hip in this unique bout, still he held tenaciously to the One who could assure him of the blessing.

I will not let You go until You guarantee to me that Your Word will be accomplished. Wrestle with me however You wish. I may walk with a limp for the rest of my life, but I will not let You go until I have what You promised me.

Jacob was in a wrestling match with God, a wrestling match in which God wanted Jacob to win in order to lay hold of the fullness of his destiny.

"What is your name?" God finally asked, in a question that would have struck Jacob to the core.

And [in shock of realization, whispering] he said, Jacob [supplanter, schemer, trickster, swindler]!

And He said, Your name shall be called no longer Jacob [supplanter], but Israel [contender with God]; for you have contended and have power with God and with men and have prevailed. . . .

Jacob called the name of the place Peniel [the face of God], saying, For I have seen God face to face, and my life is spared and not snatched away.

Genesis 32:27–28, 30 AMPC

A life-defining moment in Jacob's history. A change in his entire self-identity. He was now *Israel*, a name that has survived through all of history as the name through which redemption has come to earth. Israel, the Contender with God who prevailed; Israel, the God-wrestler who won; Israel, Prince of God; Israel, the man who held on until the blessing came.

God's Wrestlers

Jacob's night of wrestling is a significant story for us as we advance into the future. Declarations from the Lord that have lain dormant for centuries are ready to spring into reality. God is looking for wrestlers, those who will grapple with Him for the promises, who refuse to give up until the assurance comes. We may have tried prematurely to usher in those promises from God, but if they are from Him, He will bring the victory at the right time. Our role is to hold on, never to let Him go.

All Israel will be saved (Romans 11:26).

You said it Yourself, Lord. I will not let You go until all Israel—every last one of Jacob's descendants—has a revelation of the Messiah, so that Jewish people the world over are known as Jesus-followers.

159

Greater riches for the whole world when Israel comes into her fullness (see Romans 11:12).

I may walk with a limp, but I refuse to give up until Israel and the Jewish people not only have become followers of Jesus but also have entered into their intended destiny of being a light to all the nations, until every ethnic group in the world knows about this Jewish Messiah who is the world Redeemer.

In that day there will be a highway from Egypt to Assyria. The Assyrians will go to Egypt and the Egyptians to Assyria. The Egyptians and Assyrians will worship together. In that day Israel will be the third, along with Egypt and Assyria [much of the Arab world today], a blessing on the earth. The LORD Almighty will bless them, saying, "Blessed be Egypt my people, Assyria my handiwork, and Israel my inheritance" (Isaiah 19:23–25).

This is a huge promise, Lord. This has never happened, but it is written in Your Word. Arabs, Egyptians, Israelis together—a blessing in the world! Wrestle me down if You will, Lord, but I have read Your Word. I know this seems impossible today. These nations are Israel's enemies. But You have given a promise, and I hold You to Your promise. One day Egyptians and "Assyrians" will be known as followers of Your way.

Not only God's Word for world conditions but His word for each of us individually must be held tight if we are to walk out our own personal destiny. We may be "Jacobs," but we must become "Israels."

"Very truly I tell you, whoever believes in me will do the works I have been doing, and they will do even greater things than these, because I am going to the Father" (John 14:12).

I want to see blind eyes opening, the lame walking, the dead raised. When I read the stories of Your life, Jesus, I lean in to those miracles. You said I am supposed to do the same things. I have experienced a little, but I want more. I am holding on to Your promises. I will not let go until I have all of You.

If we confess our sins, he . . . will . . . purify us from all unrighteousness (1 John 1:9). We . . . are being transformed into his image with ever-increasing glory (2 Corinthians 3:18).

It's taking a long time, Lord, but Your Word is true, and I am becoming more like You. I like me better today than when You first found me, but I want more. I want to be like You. I am only repeating what You said.

God is looking for a radical firebrand remnant of believers who are not moved by the changing world or the growing wickedness around us. We, like Jacob, are holding on even when our spiritual hips (or our physical ones) have been put out of joint. This is not just another wrestling bout with men or even with demons. This is a wrestling match with God . . . and He is pulling for us to win.

And in the meantime, if we will keep on loving Him, He will work all the wrestling for our good.

15

Call on Jesus

"There is no other name under heaven given to mankind by which we must be saved."

Acts 4:12

A few months ago I had the privilege of hearing Andrew White, who at that time led a congregation of Jesus-believers in Baghdad, Iraq. He told us of a young girl in his congregation who was hospitalized and near death. The distraught father went to the clinic operated by Jesus-followers to see if they could come with him to the hospital to pray for his daughter.

When they advised him that they were not authorized to go to that hospital, he consulted Andrew, his pastor, who gave the father the following instruction: "Call on Jesus," Andrew told the father. "Speak His name continually as you leave here. Do not cease as you make your way back to your daughter. Stand over her and speak His name. There is power in the name of Jesus. Jesus! Jesus! Jesus!"

The father carefully followed the pastor's instructions. "Jesus, Jesus, Jesus!" he prayed as he left. "Jesus, Jesus, Jesus!"

as he made his way back to the hospital. "Jesus, Jesus, Jesus!" he continued as he moved ever closer to his daughter's bedside. "I commit to You the life of my daughter. Jesus!"

When the father arrived at the hospital, he was greeted with the news that the hospital staff had done everything they knew to do to save the child but to no avail. He was ushered into the room where her lifeless body lay under a sheet that had already been pulled over her head.

"Jesus, Jesus, Jesus!" the father continued to cry as he tenderly uncovered his daughter's face.

"Jesus, Jesus, Jesus!" he continued to pray, just as his pastor had instructed.

"Jesus, Jesus, Jesus!" he wept, when suddenly his daughter opened her eyes, looked into the astonished face of her father and, smiling, said, "Daddy, I'm hungry."

Call on Jesus!

The Name That Protects

A group of women gathered for a jewelry party in Florida. As they were passing around the pieces, deciding what to purchase, a masked man carrying a gun entered the house, demanding the jewelry and their purses. The hostess believed in a power greater than guns.

"Stop, in the name of Jesus!" she demanded as the thief was rifling through the ladies' handbags.

Then all the women in the room began to chant the name: "Jesus, Jesus, Jesus!"

The confused burglar dropped the purses, scattering the jewelry on the floor, and fled. Two hours later the perplexed man was apprehended by the police not far from the scene of his intended crime.[1]

Call on Jesus!

The Name That Breaks Demonic Strongholds

About eleven o'clock one night some time ago, I received a phone call from one of our young converts. (I will call him Carl.) He and his girlfriend (I will call her Suzanne), later to become his wife, were driving around, recalling events and expressing their gratitude to the Lord for redeeming them from their past when, suddenly, Suzanne became catatonic. She could not speak. Her eyes were glazed. She had lost touch with reality.

That is when Carl called me to see if he could bring Suzanne to my home for prayer. He believed that together we could break the power of the enemy and restore her to sanity.

As we began to pray the Lord gave me a picture of the battle of Ai (see Joshua 8) in which Joshua was instructed to send two separate groups of soldiers to invade enemy territory. Some would wait in ambush to descend upon the unsuspecting city from one direction. Another group would draw the men of Ai out of the city so that the battle would be approached from the opposite direction.

Carl and I were led to pray strength into Suzanne through the work of the Holy Spirit who resided within her, while at the same time asking for warring angels to descend upon and around her in the power of the Holy Spirit, freeing her from the demonic powers seeking to control her life again.

As we began to pray I asked Suzanne to call upon the name of Jesus deep within her. Her body was still rigid, her eyes fixed, but I knew that she had given her life to Jesus and that He, therefore, lived within her.

After praying for a while, giving Suzanne time to cry out for Jesus deep within the recesses of her spirit, I asked her to bring that confession into her soul—her mind, her will, her emotions—to scream His name inside her still listless body.

We stayed there for a while as Carl and I continued to pray, insisting that Suzanne cry out to Jesus.

"Now, Suzanne, begin to bring His name, the name of Jesus, across your lips," I encouraged her. "Speak His name. Call on Jesus."

With that, we saw her lips begin to move, ever so slightly, but this gave us hope to keep praying fervently. At last Suzanne began to say, ever so softly, "Jesus, Jesus, Jesus . . ." Then louder and louder until her whole body and mind were engaged, and she was smiling at us, completely herself again.

I received email from Carl and Suzanne recently. They are still avid followers of the One who has redeemed them.

Call on Jesus!

I was just learning about all this in my early days as a pastor. One morning, around 2:30, I received a phone call.

"Don, would you pray for me?" The woman on the line, whom I knew, sounded worried. "Jim just came home drunk again, and, though he has never been physically abusive to me or the children, there is something different about tonight."

I hung up the phone and began to pray. I knew all about the struggles Jim was having as a war veteran and an alcoholic. I began to wonder if I should get out of bed and go to Jim's home when the second call came from his wife.

"Don, could you come? I'm really afraid for my life."

I had learned enough about ministry to know that I must not go alone, so I called one of my covenant partners and asked if he would meet me and we would go together.

A few minutes later we parked the car and were walking toward the house when Jim came out. He appeared to be perfectly sober and apologized for bringing us out so late at night. We went inside and began to chat briefly before I laid my hand on Jim's shoulder and began to pray.

The moment I spoke the name of Jesus, Jim became a different person—a person possessed. He lunged toward me and put his hands around my neck as if to choke me.

"Don't say that, Don!" he screamed.

I am forever grateful for those times when, just as Jesus predicted to His close friends would happen, the Holy Spirit takes over my mouth and says things through me that I am not smart enough to say.

With adrenaline flowing and the peace of God amazingly saturating me, I said, "Jim, you can't touch me. I am covered by the blood of Jesus."

He sank, unconscious, at my feet. Three times that evening the same scene occurred. Another occasion when the Lord proved to me the power of His name.

Call on Jesus!

The Name That Awakens Faith

While writing this chapter I had the rare blessing of hearing Brother Yun again. As I mentioned earlier in this book, he is one of the leaders in the Chinese underground Church revival.

Brother Yun's mother had come to know Jesus during the days when Western missionaries were in China. But when Communism took control of the country, the missionaries were expelled and church buildings were destroyed. His mother had no fellowship, and her faith became dormant.

Meanwhile, she married and had six children. Brother Yun's older brother, age fifteen, died of starvation, and his father was dying of cancer. His mother, despairing of life, tied a noose around her neck and was about to take her own life when she heard an audible voice: *Don't give up! Call on Jesus.*

Remembering her faith in Jesus, she awakened her five children and told them to get up, kneel around their father's bed and call on Jesus. Though the children had never heard this name before and had no idea who this "Jesus" was, they obeyed their mother.

Within the week, the father was healed. The family began to spread the news, and the mother, though illiterate and with little Bible knowledge, became the pastor of a home church. After they had prayed for months for a Bible, the Lord delivered one to their front door. The Yun family became a part of the major awakening of faith throughout their homeland in which, for years, an estimated thirty thousand people a day have been coming to believe in Jesus.

Call on Jesus!

The Name That Is Above All Names

The name of Jesus is not some mystical mantra to be pronounced for selfish gain. In fact, that could become dangerous as the sons of Sceva learned when they began to use Jesus' name without believing in Him.

> Some Jews who went around driving out evil spirits tried to invoke the name of the Lord Jesus over those who were demon-possessed. They would say, "In the name of the Jesus whom Paul preaches, I command you to come out." Seven sons of Sceva, a Jewish chief priest, were doing this. One day the evil spirit answered them, "Jesus I know, and Paul I know about, but who are you?" Then the man who had the evil spirit jumped on them and overpowered them all. He gave them such a beating that they ran out of the house naked and bleeding.
>
> Acts 19:13–16

No, not a name to be chanted in some mystical sense, invoking a mysterious deity, but the name of a Man who is God and who alone is our redemption and our strength. There are many gods, many christs, many lords, but only one Jesus of Nazareth in whom all power in heaven and earth resides.

"Why do you stare at us as if by our own power or godliness we had made this man walk?" (Acts 3:12), Peter told the astonished crowd after the healing of the lame man at the Temple. "By faith in the name of Jesus, this man whom you see and know was made strong. It is Jesus' name and the faith that comes through him that has completely healed him, as you can all see" (verse 16). "It is by the name of Jesus Christ of Nazareth . . . that this man stands before you healed" (Acts 4:10), Peter later reported to the Sanhedrin. "There is no other name under heaven given to mankind by which we must be saved" (verse 12).

Paul wrote the Philippians that

> God exalted him to the highest place and gave him the name that is above every name, that at the name of Jesus every knee should bow, in heaven and on earth and under the earth, and every tongue acknowledge that Jesus Christ is Lord, to the glory of God the Father.
>
> Philippians 2:9–11

"You are to call him Jesus," the angel Gabriel told Miriam (Mary) when he was announcing Jesus' birth (see Luke 1:31).

We rejoice that He is our God, our Lord, our Savior, the Christ, but His *name* is Jesus (or Yeshua, which is the Hebrew form of His name and what His mother would have called Him).

At the conclusion of our prayers, we may add, "We pray in the name of Christ," or "in Your name, O God," or "in the name of the Lord." Of course, we know of whom we speak, but Scripture never directs us to pray "in God's name," "in Christ's name" or "in the name of the Lord." We are to use the name God gave His Son—Jesus.

"I will do whatever you ask in my name," (John 14:13) are Jesus' words to His disciples. "My Father will give you whatever you ask in my name. Until now you have not asked for anything in my name. . . . In that day you will ask in my name" (John 16:23–24, 26).

And Peter's message on Pentecost? "God has made this Jesus, whom you crucified, both Lord and Messiah" (Acts 2:36). Therefore, "repent and be baptized, every one of you, in the name of Jesus" (verse 38) in order to enter into the fullness of the promises.

"Whatever you do, whether in word or deed, do it all in the name of the Lord Jesus" (Colossians 3:17).

Whole worship assemblies can take place without ever speaking Jesus' name, but it is the name Jesus before whom the world will bow, the name of Jesus that every tongue will confess, the name of Jesus through which miracles will come, the name of Jesus that has been elevated above every other name.

If we would walk in His fullness and receive all the help that He has promised, we must learn to speak His name, knowing assuredly that He is the One who will turn everything for our good in these difficult last days as we love and exalt Him.

Call on Jesus!

16

Keep in Step with the Spirit

Tod McDowell

> Anyone who does not have the Spirit of Christ does not belong to him.
>
> Romans 8:9 ESV

I (Don) was baptized with the Holy Spirit in 1969, the year Tod McDowell was born. I was in my fortieth year. There was no physical manifestation at the time but a faith surrender, knowing that God speaks and that my primary role is to listen for Holy Spirit prompting and to respond in obedience.

Thirty-five years later, through the sovereign intervention of the Holy Spirit, God's call through a prophet, His confirming voice to me, then to Tod, his wife, Rachel, and their family, Tod and I began listening and walking together. This ultimately led to the McDowells' move to Nashville, where we have been in almost daily communication under the umbrella of the Holy Spirit's beckoning. Not only Tod and Rachel, but also their children—Mandy, Micah, Makai'o and Moses—listen together for instructions from God regarding ministry, travel and life. They have learned valuable lessons that are going to be more and more important for all of us as we move rapidly forward into an uncharted future. Listen prayerfully as Tod tells his story of how he came to know Jesus and how he began to hear the Holy Spirit.

Young Samuel learned to hear the voice of the Lord early in childhood while serving the prophet Eli and sleeping near the Ark of the Covenant. The Lord called to Samuel, but since he had never heard God's voice, Samuel assumed that Eli was calling.

"Here I am," Samuel said as he ran to Eli's side. "Here I am; you called me" (1 Samuel 3:5).

You probably know the rest of the story. This happened three times, before Eli realized that God was calling Samuel, that "the word of the LORD had not yet been revealed to him" (verse 7). In other words, Samuel had not learned to recognize God's voice.

"Go and lie down," Eli told Samuel, "and if he calls you say, 'Speak, LORD, for your servant is listening'" (verse 9).

Samuel returned to his place, ready to listen for God's voice.

Early Holy Spirit Encounter

I had my own first encounter with the Lord at a time when I did not recognize who was at work.

In my early years, our family was one of those classic dysfunctional, disintegrated families. I never remember my parents being together, and as a result I spent a lot of time alone, walking through woods, sleeping alone. Nights were dreaded because of the monster-like demons that filled my dreams, the grotesque images that left me paralyzed with fear. I would awaken in panic and eventually cry myself back to sleep, only to awaken again with the same horrific scenes. This happened again and again until one night, through nothing unusual that I had done, the Lord showed up and pierced my darkness. I knew nothing about God and His ways, and not until years later was I able to identify this early God-visit as a preparation for me to meet Jesus and begin to be led by His Spirit.

In the middle of one of my nightly terrors, with darkness engulfing me and horrendous creatures choking me, I felt my life slipping away. Suddenly the screen of my eight-year-old mind became bright white, brilliant white, like staring into the sun. Darkness fled. Fear was gone and there were no more demonic creatures. Something or Someone had come to save me and pull me out of the abyss. In the next moment in my dream/vision, I was sitting on a swing in my favorite park—peaceful, sunny and laughing in total freedom and perfect joy. I awoke with a sense that my life had been handed back to me. I had no idea who had so helped me, but never again did the demonic creatures return.

This power of God breaking into my darkness is available for all. I would encourage every reader to pray for the same breakthrough for family and friends who may be in similar bondage. In these last days the enemy will try to paralyze many with fear, but God's power is always greater.

One year later, through the invitation of a school friend, I walked into a small church that met in the recreation building about one hundred yards from the swing in the park of my dream. I gave my life to Jesus, was baptized in the creek about thirty yards from the swing and never turned back, even though no one in my immediate family at that time was following Jesus.

While attending a youth camp nine years later, I learned more about the work and gifts of the Holy Spirit. Hungry for more I went up for prayer for God's Holy Spirit to be released in and through me. The only way I know how to describe the difference is that I felt I advanced from a spiritual bike ride to a ride in a high-powered car.

I was experiencing what Jesus told His disciples after His resurrection and before His ascension: "You will receive power when the Holy Spirit comes on you" (Acts 1:8)—what the disciples experienced a few days later when they were "filled with the Holy Spirit and began to speak in other tongues as the Spirit enabled them" (Acts 2:4). Life has not always been a blaze of glory since that day, but I have never been the same. I am filled with an inexpressible joy of God that transcends every hardship and keeps me surrendered to His fullness in my life.

From that day forward, the power present in my childhood encounter, the power who now has a name—*Jesus*—has had my life. His Spirit is my counselor, the One who convicts me of sin, who leads me in righteousness (see John 16:8–11), my strength, my encourager and my comforter (see 1 Corinthians 14:3). "His incomparably great power . . . the same as the mighty strength he exerted when he raised Christ from the dead" (Ephesians 1:19–20) is within me. Following His Spirit is also what brought me together with Don Finto and ultimately into this message regarding the end times. I am confident of the Lord's power in me to shine His light through me in the world's darkest hours to come.

Passing the Test

Like Samuel's nighttime encounter with God when he was learning to listen to His voice, the listening sometimes has its challenging side. In Samuel's encounter, God told him about the judgment that was to come to his mentor, Eli. This was not what Samuel expected or wanted to hear but was a test as to whether or not he would be faithful to carry out God's revelation and His instructions, even when they were not his choice at all.

I have had some of those tests. You will, too, as you follow closely the voice of the Spirit.

One of my difficult encounters happened during my courtship days with Rachel. We both knew Jesus and were walking forward together, always wanting to know His will. Most of our courtship took place in worship assemblies, in hospitals and nursing homes or in ministry to the poor. After seeing each other for several months, I sensed the Holy Spirit taking our relationship to another level, and I even felt that our next time together was to be a special time of revelation for us.

I was full of expectation when I picked her up and headed for our special spot on the edge of some cliffs overlooking a bay on the coast. As we drove to our destination, I kept asking the Holy Spirit what gift He was to give us. Why was this night to be so special? But God is not on our timing, so I had to be patient.

As we walked up the steep bank to our private piece of land, my mind was racing. When we found our spot, we were surprised to find a freshly lit fire with wood burning, yet no one in sight. We looked around, but it was as though some special angel had built us a fire and left just in time for us to have the full enjoyment. I was in awe, basking in the tangible sense of the Lord's presence with my arm around the most beautiful woman I had ever met.

I began again to ask the Lord, *What is going to be so special? Is this the night of our first kiss? What are You revealing?*

At last there was an answer: *Don't kiss until your wedding day, and don't hold hands with fingers interlocking until you are engaged.*

I was undone! The voice was the voice of God, but the instructions were devastating. My first response was to rebuke the enemy. *He wants to steal the joy of this moment,* I thought. *Surely I heard wrong. I'll ask again.*

Don't kiss until marriage, and don't hold hands with fingers interlocking until you are engaged.

I was silent, allowing time for God to rearrange my heart. *Maybe this is just a test, and once I agree to be obedient, He will release me. The Lord did not make me a stoic. Surely, I have heard wrong.*

But the same phrase kept repeating inside me.

Finally in a moment of resignation and surrender, I said hesitatingly to Rachel, "What would you think if we didn't kiss until marriage and if we didn't hold hands until we were engaged?"

I expected her to laugh, but her response was immediate. "I think that's great."

I was still in a state of shock, but after a short pause I was able to look up to the heavens and say, *This is the next level in our relationship, isn't it?*

Yes, He said, and my heart was sealed.

"Whoever belongs to God hears what God says" (John 8:47), Jesus said, and affirmed it: "My sheep listen to my voice" (John 10:27).

I am not asking you to follow God's instructions for Rachel and me, but if we were going to be obedient to this God whom we knew to be the only true God and to the instructions of His Holy Spirit, if we were to experience the fullness of His joy for us, our path was now clear.

Two years and seven months later, after being separated through ministry much of the time, we kissed for the first time in front of three hundred of our closest friends and family as we sealed a life covenant together in marriage. God has been faithful to His covenant. Over 25 years of marriage and four children later, He has continued to pursue us, talk to us, change us and bless us.

And we were about to discover where He would lead us.

Like the Wind

One night Jesus was talking to Nicodemus about the work of God's Spirit. He told Nicodemus that he needed to be born again. Nicodemus had no idea what Jesus meant. "How can a man be born when he is old?" he asked (John 3:4 NKJV).

Jesus responded to Nicodemus by comparing natural birth and spiritual birth. "The Spirit gives birth to spirit," Jesus said, then proceeded to compare the Holy Spirit's work to the wind. "The wind blows wherever it pleases. You hear its sound, but you cannot tell where it comes from or where it is going. So it is with everyone born of the Spirit" (verses 6, 8).

We sometimes overlook the fact that Jesus is not only saying that the Holy Spirit is like the wind, which He is, but that this is the way "it is with everyone born of the Spirit." We are not the wind, but we respond to the Wind. We must keep our spiritual sails hoisted in order to be sure that we are responding to any redirection that may come from His Holy Spirit Wind.

Rachel and I have had a few of those experiences as well. Up until the year 2005, after having served for fifteen years in Youth With A Mission's Kona, Hawaii, base, we began to assume this would be our launching place for the rest of our lives. Our four children were born in Kona. We had traveled to many nations on outreaches. I had served on the President's Council with YWAM founders and base leaders, Loren and Darlene Cunningham. I had led in schools and taught in the biblical studies program of the University of the Nations. We had our first home. And besides all this, we were a family of surfers.

But remember that we never know where the gale force of the Holy Spirit is going to take us.

Even though our lives were full, I began to sense that there was more. I began to ask the Lord why there was still uneasiness within me. What were the keys to this world revival for which we were all yearning?

So I withdrew from all ministry for forty days so that I could give myself to prayer and fasting, seeking the Lord for greater clarity. I asked my staff to hold any calls unless they were essential, so that I could spend hours each day in worship and prayer.

On day 35 of the fast, I received a call from one of my intercessors from Australia.

"Hello, Tod, I am so grateful for what you are doing. Thank you for sending out prayer notes to me during the fast. I love what you are doing and totally agree with the revelation the Lord is giving you, but I believe you are missing a piece. I want to suggest to you that there is a key to world revival of which you may not be aware. You need to get the 'Israel piece.'"

My first response, I have to confess, was to dismiss this puzzling suggestion, get off the phone and resume my prayer and fasting for direction. But I felt I owed it to her to listen.

"What do you mean, the 'Israel piece'?" I asked, trying to show interest.

"You need to read this book by Don Finto, *Your People Shall Be My People: How Israel, the Jews and the Christian Church Will Come Together in the Last Days*," she told me.

"Oh," I responded, my tone changing. "I actually have that book. It was given to us in Singapore at a major YWAM meeting."

The call ended, and I sat there contemplating what my intercessor had just told me.

Could it be, Lord, that there is some kind of key to world revival that involves the Jewish people? Please, Lord, I want to be open to whatever You are showing me.

I was still pondering thoughts like this when, within the hour, I received another call, this time from the leader of one of our schools, a school that was actually under my supervision, the School of Jewish Studies.

"Tod, forgive me for calling," the leader said. "I know that you are not taking many calls, but we have a guest speaker on base this week. He has a free day on Friday, and I wondered if you have any desire to meet with him. His name is Don Finto."

I was stunned. This was all sounding like His voice again.

I sent up a quick prayer: *Lord, what's going on? Am I really missing something?*

"Yes," I finally responded to the leader. "I'd be glad to have some time with Don Finto."

And so it happened that Friday morning at eleven o'clock I walked into the GO Center at the Kona base and met Don Finto for the first time. He did not appear at all the way I imagined a man who carried this "Israel piece" to be. For starters, he had no prayer shawl draped around his shoulders, wore no *kippa* (Jewish "skull cap") and did not have a *shofar* (ram's horn) at his side! And his smile was disarming.

I told him about the two phone calls and asked him what all this could mean. "What is this 'Israel piece'? What does this have to do with world revival?"

With that, he took out his computer and began a PowerPoint presentation. I was interested, but nothing stirred me deeply until he hit Romans 11:12. "If their [the Jewish people's] transgression means riches for the world, and their loss [Jewish loss because they did not as a nation receive Jesus] means riches for the Gentiles, how much greater riches will their [Israel's] full inclusion bring!"

"Hold it," I said. "Read that again. Are you telling me that Jewish people coming to faith in their own Messiah will have an impact on all the nations? Is that what Paul is saying?"

He read Romans 11:12 again, then moved to verse 15: "If their rejection brought reconciliation to the world, what will their acceptance be but life from the dead?"

I still did not know for sure what I was hearing, but I suddenly knew that this verse held an answer to part of the mystery. At first glance, this seemed indeed to have a key to world revival—a time when the nations of the world come to know their Redeemer.

I interrupted Don. "Would you pray for me? I do believe there is something here that I need. Pray that God will give me His impartation."

As Don began to pray over me, I fell to the floor weeping. He sank beside me. We wept together.

Then I heard the gentle voice of the Lord: *You are married to Israel.*

Later I understood. I realized that if God is married to/in covenant with Israel, which He is, and if I am married to/in covenant with Yeshua/Jesus, which I am, then I am married to/in covenant with Israel.

The wind of the Spirit was blowing on me with a new force. I was not sure what all this meant, but I was now ready to dive into Don's book and ask for whatever revelation God intended.

One month later Don called me from Israel. Remember, we had spent only one hour together before he briefly met Rachel and the children at a gathering that evening. Now Don was calling to say that he had just received a prophetic word that he and I were to be walking together for the next season.

"I believe this word is from God," Don said. "I do not know what it means fully, but would you and Rachel pray about it and call me back?"

Two days later, after listening with the whole family and conferring with some of those who knew Don well, I called him back.

"Yes," I told him. "We do not know what all this means, either, but the answer is yes. Let's do it!"

Don and I began ministering together. We traveled to Kansas City, Nashville, Los Angeles, Redding, Kona. We journeyed to Israel, England, Turkey, Egypt, Cyprus and Korea.

The wind kept blowing across us until it became clear to my family that we were being removed from our secure base in Kona and being sent to Nashville to live near Don and his family. We were to become a part of his Caleb Company ministry, with a base in Israel plus training schools and seminars all over the world, and developing a prayer center at the base south of Nashville. I am now the director of the ministry Don founded, as we still walk in close covenant together as a father/son team.

"The wind blows wherever it pleases. You hear its sound, but you cannot tell where it comes from or where it is going. So it is with everyone who is born of the Spirit."

Life in Jesus is never boring. Sometimes momentarily excruciating, but never boring.

Holy Spirit Conviction

One of the roles of the Holy Spirit in our lives is to "convict the world concerning sin and righteousness and judgment" (John 16:8 NASB), so that we can confess those sins and enter into greater purity and wholeness (see 1 John 1:9).

Soon after my family moved from Kona to Nashville, I became convicted that I needed to let Don know of one of the sin patterns that continued to ensnare me. I never will forget the day I felt the time had come for me to broach the subject. Don and I shared an office, with desks across the room from each other. I stopped what I was doing, turned my chair toward him, held on to the sides of the chair and began, "I need to confess something to you."

The room stopped. This was a huge risk for me. I had just moved our family of six to Tennessee to work with Don, and now I was not sure he would want to continue working with me.

Carefully choosing my words, I talked to him about some of the failures that kept tripping me up. When I was finished Don got up, came over to me, knelt down, embraced me and began to speak a prayer of forgiveness and victory, pulling on heaven in a way that gave me a cleansed conscience and renewed hope. Strangely enough, he will tell you that his love and appreciation for me became even stronger that day because I had emptied myself before him, sharing my deepest needs. My life has not been flawless since that day, but I have had victories that I had never before experienced.

But confession of this sort is rarely one way. I had learned to trust Don because of his unusual life transparency, grateful for a father figure with whom I could be crassly honest.

Not long after that office encounter I received a call from Don.

"I have to see you before the day is over," he said. "There is something I need to confess to you—a pattern that has continually tripped me, and I want it broken."

You have to realize that this man is no longer a teenager (he says he is in double overtime; he is past eighty), but he is still determined to grow up into the image of Jesus. Perhaps he could have become victorious without his confession to me, but this kind of one-another-ness has enhanced our ability to walk together. We keep clean slates with each other and with others, are quick to confess and quick to forgive. Don has helped me to become a better husband to Rachel and father to my children, never putting ministry above family.

The Holy Spirit is an excellent "Convict-er." He may use people—an evangelist, a teacher, a pastor—but without the Holy Spirit's work there is no conviction of sin. I may not like the moment of conviction, but I love what God is making of me as I cooperate with Him.

Our primary role in life is to listen to the Spirit and respond in obedience. As we move into the future that will contain the world's greatest wickedness as well as the world's greatest righteousness, it is essential that we are open to the fullness of the Holy Spirit.

He will always guide into truth (see John 16:13), never in contradiction to the revealed Word given us in Scripture, and He will always come in gentleness.

When the Holy Spirit descended on Jesus at His baptism, He came "like a dove" (Luke 3:22). This is significant. He did not come like a hawk or an eagle, but a dove. A dove is a non-aggressive, gentle bird. I interacted with them many times while living in Hawaii. Gentleness and calm attract them. Busyness and activity repel them. We must often halt our much activity to attract the Holy Spirit. Then we will enter into the grandest outpouring of the Holy Spirit in history.

"I will pour out my Spirit on all people" is the prophecy given through Joel (Joel 2:28).

"I will put my Spirit in you and move you to follow my decrees and be careful to keep my laws," God affirms through Ezekiel (Ezekiel 36:27).

"Rivers of living water will flow from within [you]" (John 7:38), Jesus promises.

You will "shine among them like stars in the sky as you hold firmly to the word of life" (Philippians 2:15), Paul proclaims.

These are His promises, and they fill us with hope for the days ahead.

17

Live in Community

Be devoted to one another in love.

Romans 12:10

The two scenes are still very vivid in my memory—two families, two completely different scenarios. One is the sight of dozens, even hundreds, crowding into a hospital chapel for prayer, lingering in the hallways outside the room of a young mother and wife whose life was hanging in the balance. The other is the picture of a near-vacant parking lot, an empty funeral home and a couple standing alone in front of an open coffin.

The first scene followed a tragic accident. The young woman was hovering between life and death in intensive care. The waiting room, chapel and parking lots were filled to capacity with praying, warring, loving friends, young and old. Those present had frequented each other's homes and visited together in prayer meetings, Bible studies and soccer games. Birthday celebrations and weddings, baby showers and vacations were common occasions. They loved each other with devotion reserved for the followers of Jesus. Not all were in the same room on Sunday morning, but during the week they connected in a relational, supportive, encouraging community of like-minded believers in Jesus.

The second scene followed the death of the father/father-in-law of one of the couples who attended our congregation regularly. I was not sure how many people even knew about it. I wanted to be present, partially because I was concerned that the couple, though reasonably well-known, longtime residents in the city and members of the church, stayed pretty much to themselves. Their home was generally devoid of friends. Birthdays and holidays were rarely times of celebration.

I drove to the funeral home and found that, indeed, the parking lot was empty but for their car and mine. I walked in to find the couple alone beside the coffin in the corner of the room. This couple attended the Sunday morning gatherings consistently, but they did not live in community. Sitting in a pew, singing together and listening to the messages week after week does not produce community.

"Church" Is Togetherness

"Church" is an unfortunate mistranslation of the Greek word *ekklesia*—literally meaning "called out." The Greek word carries no connotation of a building but of people.

William Tyndale understood this. In his 1525 completed text of the New Testament, there is no *church*; there is only *community*. Even under great pressure to translate *ekklesia* as "church," Tyndale resisted and translated with the best word he could find in the English language for the translation of *ekklesia*—"community."[1]

Martin Luther had the same problem. As he was defying the church in translating Scripture by using the original texts as nearly as he could, he refused the German word *kirche* (church) in favor of the word *gemeinde* (community) for translating *ekklesia*. There is no *church* in Luther's German Bible. Luther understood that *community* is different from *church*.[2]

Under the oversight of King James of England almost a century later, the translators forsook Tyndale's definition and used the word that more aptly described the conditions of the early seventeenth century Church of England. After all, King James was the official head of the Church of England, and the Church of England knew only cathedrals and buildings as the center for Christians.[3]

Daniel Gruber was attempting to drive this point home in the first volume of *The Separation of Church and Faith* in the chapter entitled "A Good Church Is Hard to Find." He shockingly but accurately states,

> There is no "church" in the Biblical text. The "Church" is not the Biblical *ekklesia*. Every time you see the word "church" in a Bible, you are seeing a place where the translators did not translate the text, but distorted it instead, for the sake of tradition. Often it is done without thinking about it, simply because the hold of Christian tradition is so strong.[4]
>
> . . . Whatever the case may be, "assembly," "congregation," and "community" are adequate translations of *ekklesia* in the biblical context. "Church" is not a translation. It is an invention that replaces proper translation. It gives a meaning which is not contained in *ekklesia*. It conveys a concept that is not in the Scriptures.[5]

Jesus came to redeem a people separated to Himself, a people who live in community with each other and love each other with a love that only God can produce and which serves to draw others into the Kingdom. The biblical record tells us that in the middle of the persecution of those early days, "more and more men and women believed in the Lord and were added to their number" (Acts 5:14).

Tyndale and Luther both knew that the New Covenant emphasis was not gatherings in specially constructed buildings, since church buildings did not make their appearance until the third or early fourth century. They knew that the *ekklesia* is the body of people who are committed to the God of Abraham, Isaac and Jacob, and to His Promised Messiah who has been revealed to us through the Holy Spirit.

We may object to this distinction being made regarding the translation of *ekklesia,* and we may insist that we have never intended to imply that the "church" is a building. A very large percentage of those who understand the difference, however, and who vigorously defend the "church" as the people, still refer to buildings as "churches": "We leave for church every Sunday at about ten," they say, or, pointing to a building, "That's the (whatever denomination) church."

Early Believers Met in Homes

Believers, in the early centuries after Jesus, did not have this problem as it relates to fine buildings. Nor do the people of God in the persecuted areas of the world today.

"They broke bread in their homes," Luke tells us (Acts 2:46). When Saul was looking for believers in Jesus, he did not try to find meetings in church buildings. There were none. He went "from house to house [dragging] off both men and women and [putting] them in prison" (Acts 8:3).

Peter, after being miraculously released from prison, went to a place he must have known was a favorite gathering place for believers. Indeed, He found an all-night prayer meeting in the home of John Mark's mother, Mary (see Acts 12:12).

Paul continually sent greetings to the community of believers: "Aquila and Priscilla greet you warmly in the Lord, and so does the church that meets at their house" (1 Corinthians 16:19); "Give my greetings . . . to Nympha and the church in her house" (Colossians 4:15); "To Philemon . . . and to the church that meets in your home" (Philemon 1–2).

We in the West often have some of the finest homes in the world, yet we build superstructures as the meeting places for believers, rather than using our homes as was done in the early centuries.

Even in our day in the areas of the world where the Gospel of Jesus is advancing most rapidly, usually there are no buildings and no paid clergy. More often, the people of God are being harassed, arrested, imprisoned and even killed for their faith. Believers gather in small assemblies, sometimes even mouthing hymns so as not to awaken the curiosity of neighbors who could call the police.

In my office there is a cherished, framed picture of a Communion service in a forest—an open-air assembly being held secretly during the reign of Communism in Eastern Europe. A brother who lived through that era in Eastern Europe told me that at times no word of any kind could be sent out to notify the congregation where they would meet next, lest the message be intercepted by the secret police and some or all be arrested and imprisoned. Each member had to listen for the Holy Spirit's directions in order to find the next meeting place.

Many of us in the West are aware that we may one day find ourselves in similar circumstances. We may be forced into real community before the return of Jesus. This happened when Communism began its reign in China. Church buildings were destroyed. Leaders were dispersed and often killed. If such a situation should arise in the West, we may learn who are the true disciples of Jesus and who are simply culturally Christian.

Restoring Community

All of this reminds me of one of the significant times in the life of Jesus when He was being barraged with questions. More often than not, He did not answer the questions directly, often replying with another question. On one occasion, this was not the case.

A group of Pharisees had observed Jesus for days and sought eagerly to find a question that would trip Him up so that His answer could be used against Him. Knowing that all of God's commandments are important, one of the Pharisees came up with a trick question: "Teacher, which is the greatest commandment in the Law?" (Matthew 22:36).

In other words, "We all know that there are 613 commandments, and surely You know that they are all of equal importance, so how are You going to respond to this one? What do You think? Which one is most important?"

Without hesitation, Jesus replied,

> "The most important one is this: 'Hear, O Israel: the Lord our God, the Lord is one. Love the Lord your God with all your heart and with all your soul and with all your mind and with all your strength.' The second is this: 'Love your neighbor as yourself.' There is no commandment greater than these. . . . All the Law and the Prophets hang on these two commandments."
>
> Mark 12:29–31; Matthew 22:40

The Pharisee who asked the question was so surprised by Jesus' reply that, before he had time to think, he blurted in front of his fellow Pharisees,

> "Well said, teacher. You are right in saying that God is one and there is no other but him. To love him with all your heart, with all your understanding and with all your strength, and to

love your neighbor as yourself is more important than all burnt offerings and sacrifices."

Mark 12:32–33

In other words, "I would never have thought of it this way, but, of course, if we love God with all our hearts, and if we love our neighbors as ourselves, then we will obey all of God's laws. We will have no other gods, we will not make idols, we will not take His name in vain, we will honor His holy day, and we will treat others well, honoring our parents, never murdering, stealing, lying or coveting" (see Exodus 20:1–17).

Jesus' answer to the Pharisee was a call to keep God in proper priority and to live in community with each other. His was not a call to build elaborate cathedrals in His honor or to spend billions of dollars having the finest all-purpose campuses in the world. He did not call us to once-a-week meetings in those houses. He did not have in mind that we would sit for hours listening to a man or woman bring a nice, even challenging message. He was not even primarily interested in our production of the most awesome worship music the world has ever known. Some of these things may come as an outworking of our love for God and for each other, but if we replace the first and second Commandments with anything, including any of the above, we have digressed from the very reason Jesus came—to restore us to God the Father and to restore us to each other.

I am grieved each time I hear of another pastor or television personality who has had a moral failure, but I am also convinced that, though these men and women may have been in "church" all of their lives, many of them have never lived in "community." I would dare also to say that disciples of Jesus who live in God-intended community will not experience moral or ethical failure. Why? Because they are accountable to others who live close to them and help them to stay aware of dangers.

We can live all our lives in "church" and never know "community," never know *ekklesia*.

Love God, Love One Another

We see this example of loving God and loving each other continuing in the lives of the early apostles and disciples. Paul and the other writers of Scripture often break wide open in praise to God before they even state the reason for their letter.

"Praise be to the God and Father of our Lord Jesus Christ" (2 Corinthians 1:3).

"Praise be to the God and Father of our Lord Jesus Christ, who has blessed us in the heavenly realms with every spiritual blessing in Christ" (Ephesians 1:3; see also Galatians 1:3–5; Colossians 1:15–17; 1 Peter 1:3–4; 2 Peter 1:3).

These believers had their priorities established. First priority, first Commandment: Love God.

In the same way apostolic writings are filled with the challenge to relate lovingly to each other. Second priority, second Commandment: Love each other.

"Dear friends, let us love one another, for love comes from God. Everyone who loves has been born of God and knows God . . . since God so loved us, we also ought to love one another" (1 John 4:7, 11; see also Romans 12:10–16; 2 Corinthians 13:11 and many other Scriptures).

Keep the priorities: Love God; love each other. Live in one-another-ness. Live in community.

Be sure that "church" for you does not push out "community." If you are not walking with a few close friends in the Kingdom, friends who will challenge you to live closer to God, friends to whom you confess sins and ask for prayer, friends who confess their sins and their needs to you and receive your prayer, if you are not walking in the light with a few close friends, then you may have been in church all your life, may even be on the front row of the larger assemblies every week, but you are not living in that to which Jesus has called us.

This need for genuine community will only heighten as we experience the ripening of both evil and righteousness. There may come a time in our own nation, as is true in many nations, when public assemblies of believers are not allowed. Only those who are moving forward with a priority of loving God and loving each other in tangible and life-transforming ways will have strength to survive, and even to thrive. They will continue to walk in the confidence and joy reserved for Jesus-followers, knowing that, in the end, everything has worked for our good.

18

Raise Up the Generations

Now teach these truths to other trustworthy people who
will be able to pass them on to others.

2 Timothy 2:2 NLT

One of my favorite stories in the Bible (I have many) is the story
of the younger Joshua leading the fight against the Amalekites
in the valley while three old men were up on the mountain praying. At least, I assume they were praying. They were watching
the battle and Moses, perhaps involuntarily, was lifting up his
hands as he watched.

Moses said to Joshua, "Choose some of our men and go out
to fight the Amalekites. Tomorrow I will stand on top of the
hill with the staff of God in my hands."
So Joshua fought the Amalekites as Moses had ordered, and
Moses, Aaron and Hur went to the top of the hill. As long as
Moses held up his hands, the Israelites were winning, but when-
ever he lowered his hands, the Amalekites were winning. When
Moses' hands grew tired, they took a stone and put it under him
and he sat on it. Aaron and Hur held his hands up—one on one

side, one on the other—so that his hands remained steady till sunset. So Joshua overcame the Amalekite army with the sword.

Exodus 17:9–13

I may be reading more into the story than is here, but I visualize the scene when Moses catches on to what is happening—hands high, the battle being won; hands drooping, the battle being lost. I even wonder if Moses may have called to Aaron and Hur, saying, "Watch this!" then showed them—hands up, battle won; hands down, battle lost.

As Aaron and Hur caught the picture, they grabbed that stone and set Moses on it so that they could hold up his hands until "Joshua overcame the Amalekites."

Why so interesting to me? Because the victory could not be accomplished simply by the young men fighting in the valley. They needed the old men on the hill, even if all they did was to hold up Moses' hands. But the old men would never have defeated the Amalekites without the younger people involved in the battle.

I have also been fascinated with God's instructions to Moses after the battle was over. "Write this on a scroll as something to be remembered and make sure that Joshua hears it, because I will completely blot out the name of Amalek from under heaven" (Exodus 17:14).

"Make sure Joshua hears it. Joshua needs to know that the generations had to be joined for the battle to be won. Write this on a scroll as something to be remembered. Tell the story over and over again."

Young and old must appreciate each other and walk together if we are to be successful and victorious.

Faithful Since His Youth

We would also do well to consider some of the reasons God may have chosen Joshua to be the future leader of Israel.

Joshua "had been Moses' aide since youth" (Numbers 11:28), even setting out with Moses when he "went up on the mountain of God" to receive the two tablets God inscribed with the Ten Commandments (Exodus 24:12–13; see also Deuteronomy 1:38), obviously observing Moses, shadowing him, watching him.

Yet Joshua was more interested in the Presence of God than friendship with Moses. "The LORD would speak to Moses face to face, as one speaks to a friend. Then Moses would return to the camp, but his young aide Joshua son of Nun did not leave the tent" (Exodus 33:11).

Joshua stayed in the tent, basking in the Presence of God.

No surprise then that Joshua was selected as one of the twelve who would spy out the land. He was given a place of responsibility and authority to test his faithfulness to God when given a task (see Numbers 13:16). He carried out his duties well in the face of opposition from ten of the twelve men sent out together and ultimately the wrath of the entire community of Israel who talked of stoning them. Only he and Caleb, of all the men twenty years old and older who left Egypt, were allowed to enter the land of promise (see Numbers 32:11–12).

Who then would God ordain as the next leader? One who had been beside the leader even since youth; one who stayed behind at the "tent of God's Presence"; one who had been faithful to carry out assigned tasks with care and excellence.

Joshua was the obvious heir apparent. "Take Joshua son of Nun, a man in whom is the spirit of leadership, and lay your hand on him," God instructed Moses. "Have him stand before Eleazar the priest and the entire assembly and commission him in their presence. Give him some of your authority so the whole Israelite community will obey him" (Numbers 27:18–20). "Commission [him], and encourage and strengthen him, for he will lead this people across and will cause them to inherit the land that you will see" (Deuteronomy 3:28).

Thus, "Joshua son of Nun was filled with the spirit of wisdom because Moses had laid his hands on him" (Deuteronomy 34:9). Joshua received wisdom, authority and power from the Lord because Moses laid his hands on him. This is the godly impartation of the older generation to the next.

Blessing of the Fathers

To the nation of Israel, Moses later said,

> "The LORD your God himself will cross over ahead of you. . . . Joshua also will cross over ahead of you, as the LORD said. . . ." Then Moses summoned Joshua and said to him in the presence of all Israel, "Be strong and courageous, for you must go with this people into the land that the LORD swore to their ancestors to give them. . . . The LORD himself goes before you and will be with you; he will never leave you nor forsake you. Do not be afraid; do not be discouraged."
>
> Deuteronomy 31:3, 7–8

"And Moses the servant of the LORD died there in Moab. . . . [and] the Israelites grieved for Moses in the plains of Moab thirty days" (Deuteronomy 34: 5, 8).

At the end of the thirty-day period of grieving, the Lord appeared to Joshua. "Moses my servant is dead," He said. "Now then, you and all these people, get ready to cross the Jordan River into the land I am about to give to them" (Joshua 1:2).

I find it slightly humorous that God told Joshua, "Moses is dead." He knew that. The entire community had mourned him for thirty days. But God wanted Joshua to accept the full impact of Moses' death. Leadership had now passed into Joshua's hands.

> "As I was with Moses, so I will be with you. . . . Be strong and courageous. . . . Keep this Book of the Law always on your

lips; meditate on it day and night, so that you may be careful
to do everything written in it. Then you will be prosperous
and successful."

Joshua 1:5–6, 8

And the people's response to Joshua? "Just as we fully obeyed
Moses, so we will obey you. Only may the LORD your God be
with you as he was with Moses" (Joshua 1:17).

Passing the Torch

This principle permeates Scripture and will be increasingly
important as we move into the turbulent days ahead. "The
things you have heard me say in the presence of many witnesses
entrust to reliable people who will also be qualified to teach
others," Paul told Timothy (2 Timothy 2:2). "Go and make
disciples of all nations . . . teaching them to obey everything
I have commanded you," Jesus instructed the Twelve shortly
before His departure (Matthew 28:19–20).

In other words, "Keep passing down the mantle of leadership
and authority. Raise up the generations behind you. Join them
together as one. Empower them. Charge them."

To win the battles in any generation, the wisdom, faithfulness and maturity of the old must be partnered with the zeal,
passion and energy of the young.

For more than 25 years I served as the senior pastor, the
point leader, of a community of believers in Nashville, Tennessee. During the last few years of the pastorate, during my
annual reading through Scripture, I was repeatedly arrested by
a strange little verse in the book of Numbers, where God tells
Moses to tell Aaron to assign the Levites work in the Tent of
Meeting from their 25th to their 50th years. At the age of fifty,
they were no longer to do the work themselves, but were to
assist others who were doing it (see Numbers 8:24–25).

Here was a principle God was imparting to me: If we, as older leaders, insist on holding on to our positions of authority into old age, we will ultimately release leadership to a generation that has not been prepared to lead. In the later years of our lives, our role is to empower the next generations, releasing both responsibility and authority to them, while serving with them for both encouragement and counsel.

This kind of intergenerational relationship is imperative in the perilous, yet glorious years ahead, the younger receiving wisdom from the older, the older enjoying the strength and vitality of the younger—and God working it all for everyone's good.

19

Prophesy Life to Yourself

> For we are God's handiwork, created in Christ Jesus to do
> good works, which God prepared in advance for us to do.
>
> Ephesians 2:10

Another imperative for vibrant living in the last days is to grasp God's perception of ourselves rather than our own perception of who we are. Who are we in God's eyes? How are we gifted? What is His desire for us? Are we willing to forego our own opinions of ourselves in favor of God's higher calling? Look at the differences in the ways some of God's heroes of the past were called to grander vision.

A Non-Leader?

When God called Moses to leave the Midianite desert and return to Egypt to confront the pharaoh, he replied, "Who am I that I should go to Pharaoh and bring the Israelites out of Egypt?" (Exodus 3:11). In spite of his years of training in Pharaoh's court, Moses no longer saw himself as a leader.

"Suppose I go to the Israelites and say to them, 'The God of your fathers has sent me to you,' and they ask me, 'What is his name?' Then what shall I tell them?" (Exodus 3:13).

"What if they do not believe me or listen to me and say, 'The LORD did not appear to you'?" (Exodus 4:1).

"I have never been eloquent, neither in the past nor since you have spoken to your servant. I am slow of speech and tongue" (Exodus 4:10).

"Please send someone else" (Exodus 4:13).

Moses' impression of his identity fell far short of God's vision for him. Indeed, life had been dangerous for Moses when he had fled Egypt forty years earlier, and he had grown accustomed to his lot as a shepherd on the backside of the desert. Now things were changing . . . and he did not feel up to the assignment.

Wimp or Warrior?

Gideon had the same problem. For seven years Midian had been harassing Israel. "Because the power of Midian was so oppressive, the Israelites prepared shelters for themselves in mountain clefts, caves and strongholds" (Judges 6:2). Gideon was threshing wheat in a winepress when the angel of the Lord appeared to him. "The LORD is with you, mighty warrior" (Judges 6:12).

Mighty warrior? Hiding in a winepress?

But God does not see us as we see ourselves.

Too Young?

Listen to Jeremiah's call:

God: "Before I formed you in the womb I knew you, before you were born I set you apart; I appointed you as a prophet to the nations."

199

Jeremiah: "Alas, Sovereign LORD, I do not know how to speak; I am too young."

God: "Do not say, 'I am too young.' You must go to everyone I send you to and say whatever I command you."

Jeremiah: "Then the LORD reached out his hand and touched my mouth and said to me, 'I have put my words in your mouth. See, today I appoint you over nations and kingdoms to uproot and tear down, to destroy and overthrow, to build and to plant'" (see Jeremiah 1:5–10).

God was restoring Jeremiah's identity so that he could receive the vision He had for him. Jeremiah had a false identity of himself based on his own feelings and emotions rather than the word of God.

Overlooked or Overcomer?

What about David? David is our hero, the giant-killer, God-focused, God-warrior, always striding confidently forth in the strength of the Lord.

Or maybe not. David was the youngest of Jesse's eight sons. He was the one left in the field with the sheep when God told Samuel to invite Jesse and his sons to the sacrifice and anoint, from among his sons, the future king of Israel (see 1 Samuel 16:3).

Jesse brought seven of his sons before Samuel, but none was selected.

"Are these all the sons you have?" Samuel asked.

"There is still the youngest," Jesse answered. "He is tending the sheep."

And there, before the watching eyes of his seven older brothers and his father, David was anointed the future king of Israel.

Some believe that David was an illegitimate son, perhaps a son of a handmaiden. After all, years later David did say,

"Behold, I was brought forth in iniquity, and in sin my mother conceived me" (Psalm 51:5 NASB).

Seemingly no one in David's family saw in David what God saw. God was calling David to His/God's identity, rather than the identity David believed about himself, or the identity placed on him by family members, including his father.

This anointing from the prophet must have permeated David's life and thoughts. No wonder he could go so confidently into the battle against Goliath, fight later against all of Israel's enemies and even escape the intrigues of King Saul. After all, if God, through the prophet, had told him that he was to become the next king of Israel, he knew that he would not be killed. Was he standing on the word of the prophet? It would seem so.

David could easily have gone through life with a father wound. Indeed, he had been rejected by his father when the prophet had told Jesse to present his sons. But no father wound would control David's life. "Though my father and mother forsake me, the LORD will receive me," he would later write (Psalm 27:10). "I remain confident of this: I will see the goodness of the LORD in the land of the living" (verse 13).

David had found his identity in the words of the Lord and would ultimately walk in the fullness of God's vision for his life.

Look in the Mirror

Many of us have had less than the best of circumstances in life, and even those of us who have had the most encouraging supporters still need the full restoration of identity that can come only from God. We need to listen to God's voice and speak prophetically over ourselves.

Some years ago I began to be motivated more and more by God's description of me rather than the warped description of myself that had been a part of my plagued-with-an-inferiority-complex youth. I began to discover promises that applied to me and speak them over myself, sometimes standing in front of a mirror, admonishing myself to receive the Word of God.

I remember when I caught hold of the truth in Ephesians 1:19–20—that the very same power that raised Jesus from the dead now works in me!

I was stunned, but I began to speak this truth out loud over and over again.

I would stand before my mirror and say, "You have the resurrection power of Jesus working in you."

Then I would say to me, "But I don't feel like it!" to which I would respond with great vigor, "I did not ask you what you feel like! I am telling you what the Word of God says about you."

Speak Life

We require our Caleb students[1] to write their own vision statements, and we encourage them to continue to speak them over themselves. I have personally found that I need both an identity and a vision statement—an identity statement based entirely on the words of Scripture, and a vision statement that describes the role I play at this time in my life. Do you mind if I share them with you? Maybe this will inspire you to write your own.

This is how I now state my identity. Sometimes when I am not having the best day I have great difficulty saying this, but I still stand solidly on these truths.

- *I believe the Word of God more than I believe my own emotions or feelings; therefore, I declare boldly that I am becoming more like Jesus every day (see Romans 8:29 and 2 Corinthians 3:18).*

- *I am righteous in His sight; therefore, I have a secure future. I do not dwell on the past but embrace everything God is doing in this generation and my role in it.*

- *I have a heart after God like David (see 1 Kings 14:8; Acts 13:36); therefore, like David, I will not depart from this life until God has accomplished His purpose for me in this generation.*

- *I live in constant expectation and confidence that the Kingdom of God is advancing around the world, that Jewish people are coming to faith every day, and that the Good News of Jesus is going forth to the remotest areas of the globe.*

- *I fear the Lord and find great delight in His commands; therefore, my children will be mighty in the land. I will spend my days in prosperity, and my descendants will inherit the land (see Psalm 112).*

- *All of this will come to pass because Jesus has been given all authority in heaven and on earth, and He is my King (see Matthew 28:18).*

That is my identity, but it speaks little about my role now that I am well past the seventy and eighty landmarks. So this is how I define my vision. This helps me make decisions on what I do and do not do.

- *The primary role of my life in these latter years is to be a father to my family, extended family and others, and to be a prophetic apostolic voice to the people of God, especially those called to leadership, challenging them through who I am, what I say, write and do, to be radically sold out to Jesus all the days of their lives, and to enter into the fullness of God's destiny for them at this point in their lives with the help and power of the Holy Spirit.*

Do you see how this helps? God is not interested in our perceptions of ourselves. He wants us to walk in our God-identity and the vision He has for us. Who does *He* say I am?

I do not want to be hesitant like Moses, Gideon or Jeremiah. I want to have the God-confidence of David. I want to respond with positive action to everything God has for me. I want to be powerful and strong even in the hurricane winds of oppression, persecution, hardship or danger. I want to walk confidently into the storms to rescue those who are at risk even if it should mean that my life is given in the process. I choose not to be concerned for my own safety as long as I am walking confidently in His will. Everything is working for my good. Regardless of age, the best is always in the future.

20

Finish Well

I have fought the good fight, I have finished the race, I
have kept the faith.

2 Timothy 4:7

There are portions of Scripture that I dread reading. I know
what is coming. I have read them before, and I do not want to
read them again. One of those Scriptures is 1 Kings 11:1–6, a
description of the closing days of King Solomon's life.

Solomon had an auspicious beginning. God appeared to
Solomon shortly after he ascended the throne of Israel and
instructed him to ask for "whatever you want me to give you"
(1 Kings 3:5).

Solomon's reply is a model of humility: "I am only a little
child and do not know how to carry out my duties. . . . So give
your servant a discerning heart to govern your people and to
distinguish between right and wrong" (1 Kings 3:7, 9).

God's answer?

"Since you have asked for this and not for long life or wealth for yourself, nor have asked for the death of your enemies but for discernment in administering justice, I will do what you have asked. I will give you a wise and discerning heart, so that there will never have been anyone like you, nor will there ever be. Moreover, I will give you what you have not asked for—both wealth and honor."

1 Kings 3:11–13

Fast forward seven chapters—past the wise ruling regarding the two prostitutes who were claiming the same child as their son, past the visit of the Queen of Sheba, past the building of the Temple, past bringing the Ark of the Covenant into the Temple and placing it properly in the holy of holies, past the cloud of God's Presence so thick that "the priests could not perform their service because of the cloud, for the glory of the LORD filled his temple" (1 Kings 8:11), past Solomon's humble prayer dedicating the Temple and God's response to him, promising him that his prayer had been heard and that God's own "eyes and heart will always be there" (1 Kings 9:3)—past all this. Then move over to 1 Kings 11 and prepare for your heart to sink as you read:

"King Solomon, however, loved many foreign women. . . . His wives turned his heart after other gods. . . . So Solomon did evil in the eyes of the LORD; he did not follow the LORD completely as David his father had done" (1 Kings 11:1, 4, 6).

What happened?

Lust was clearly his downfall, but there seem to have been a number of compromises before those at the close of his life.

Words of Warning

Moses warned about the very things that tripped up Solomon. Listen to Moses' admonition:

"When you enter the land the LORD your God is giving you and have taken possession of it and settled in it, and you say, 'Let us set a king over us like all the nations around us'. . . . When he takes the throne of his kingdom, he is to write for himself on a scroll a copy of this law, taken from that of the Levitical priests. It is to be with him, and he is to read it all the days of his life so that he may learn to revere the LORD his God and follow carefully all the words of this law and these decrees and not consider himself better than his fellow Israelites and turn from the law to the right or to the left."

Deuteronomy 17:14, 18–20

Solomon was to "read [the scroll] all the days of his life." He was to "follow carefully all the words" of God's laws and decrees. He was not to "consider himself better than his brothers."

But Solomon became distracted through the very blessings God gave him. If only Solomon had listened to Moses! His warnings were precise.

Moses said . . .

"The king . . . must not acquire great numbers of horses for himself or make the people return to Egypt to get more of them, for the Lord has told you. 'You are not to go back that way again.'"

Deuteronomy 17:16

But . . .

Solomon accumulated chariots and horses; he had fourteen hundred chariots and twelve thousand horses. . . . Solomon's horses were imported from Egypt. . . . [He] imported a chariot from Egypt for six hundred shekels of silver, and a horse for a hundred and fifty.

1 Kings 10:26, 28–29

Moses said . . .

"[The king must not] accumulate large amounts of silver and gold."

Deuteronomy 17:17

But . . .

The weight of the gold that Solomon received yearly was 666 talents, not including the revenues from merchants and traders and from all the Arabian kings and the governors of the territories. King Solomon made two hundred large shields of hammered gold; six hundred shekels of gold went into each shield. He also made three hundred small shields of hammered gold, with three minas of gold in each shield. . . . Then the king made a great throne covered with ivory and overlaid with fine gold. . . . All King Solomon's goblets were gold, and all the household articles in the Palace of the Forest of Lebanon were pure gold. . . . Once every three years [a fleet of trading ships] returned, carrying gold, silver. . . . The king made silver as common in Jerusalem as stones.

1 Kings 10:14–18, 21–22, 27

Moses said . . .

"[The king] must not take many wives, or his heart will be led astray."

Deuteronomy 17:17

But . . . you know the story . . .

[Solomon] had seven hundred wives of royal birth and three hundred concubines, and his wives led him astray. As Solomon grew old, his wives turned his heart after other gods, and his heart was not fully devoted to the LORD his God. . . . He followed Ashtoreth the goddess of the Sidonians, and Molek the detestable god of the Ammonites. So Solomon did evil in the eyes of the LORD. . . . On a hill east of Jerusalem, Solomon built a high place for Chemosh the detestable god of Moab, and for Molek the detestable god of the Ammonites. He did the same for all his foreign wives, who burned incense and offered sacrifices to their gods.

1 Kings 11:3–8

Solomon followed Ashtoreth and Molek? In case you happen not to remember, Molek was worshiped through child sacrifice; Ashtoreh, through the most perverse forms of sexual immorality.

Solomon started out strong, humble—with wisdom that was unsurpassed. He ended his life as an evil, depraved idolater.

"The LORD became angry with Solomon because his heart had turned away from the LORD, the God of Israel, who had appeared to him twice" (1 Kings 11:9).

Others Who Did Not Finish Well

The biblical accounts of God's principal characters give us repeated examples and warnings of once faithful God-followers who did not finish well.

Solomon's son Rehoboam was a rebel. Grandson Abijah was even worse. "He committed all the sins his father had done before him; his heart was not fully devoted to the LORD his God, as the heart of David his forefather had been" (1 Kings 15:3).

Asa, Solomon's great-grandson, was different. He had a remarkable godly beginning. He

did what was right in the eyes of the LORD, as his father David had done. He expelled the male shrine prostitutes from the land and got rid of all the idols his ancestors had made. He even deposed his grandmother . . . because she had made a repulsive image for the worship of Asherah.

1 Kings 15:11–13

High places were removed. When a foreign army marched out against Judah, Asa turned to the Lord in prayer, and was saved from his enemy.

But in the 36th year of Asa's reign, something happened. The king of Israel marched out against him, and Asa turned to neighboring Syria for help rather than calling on the Lord. Hanani the prophet confronted him. Asa was unrepentant and angry. He had Hanani thrown into prison. Three years later, Asa "was afflicted with a disease in his feet. Though his disease was severe, even in his illness he did not seek help from the LORD, but only from the physicians" (2 Chronicles 16:12). A year later he was dead.

Asa did not finish well.

On Guard

Lust . . . greed . . . pride—lurking near all of us. "Be on your guard," warn both Paul and Peter (1 Corinthians 16:13; 2 Peter 3:17). "If you think you are standing firm, be careful that you don't fall!" (1 Corinthians 10:12).

I have seen too many men and women who started strong but stumbled severely before the finish line. I remember well the days of the Jesus Movement in the late '60s and early '70s. I can still see some of those passionate new disciples who were baptized in swimming pools, bathtubs and rivers. I have lain on floors alongside them, praying until the early morning hours. I have sat for hours in their dorm rooms, in parks and in coffee shops. I have looked into their eyes and seen the yearning for the fullness of God and watched as they drank in the Holy Spirit through whom they overcame the most debilitating of drug and alcohol addictions, illicit sexual cravings and other godlessness. I have listened to the songs that were born of their passionate faith.

I am grateful still to be walking with many of those who never lost the fire. They are more zealous for the things of God today than in those early Jesus Movement days. They are yearning for more and are being used by God all over the world.

But I have also watched as, through the years, the fervor of many has grown cold. Some have returned, as Peter would say, like a dog to their own "vomit," like "a sow that is washed returns to her wallowing in the mud" (2 Peter 2:22). They are following the example of Solomon and his sons who, in surrendering to their own lust, greed and pride, have forsaken the King.

I also grieve over public figures—television evangelists, pastors of great churches and others—who seemed to walk with great passion for Jesus but were later found to have lived lives of hypocrisy. Peter described them as "bold and arrogant," experts in greed who "exploit you with fabricated stories. Their condemnation has long been hanging over them. . . . [They] despise authority [and] with eyes full of adultery, they never stop sinning; they seduce the unstable" (2 Peter 2:3, 10, 14).

Unfortunately, these stories are not all that unusual. A few years ago when one of our well-known pastors in Nashville was discovered in an adulterous affair with his secretary, I got on the phone immediately and called all the young pastors I could think of, assuring them that this did not have to describe their own lives, that they could know a power of God through His Spirit that could overcome every temptation.

Walking Strong

Thank God, we can finish well, no matter what we have done or where we have been.

The biblical Simeon was "righteous and devout. He was waiting for the consolation of Israel, and the Holy Spirit was on him" (Luke 2:25). When he saw the infant Jesus in the arms of His parents, he walked over to Joseph and Mary, took the Child into his arms, and said, "Sovereign Lord, as you have promised, you may now dismiss your servant in peace. For my eyes have seen your salvation, which you have prepared in the sight of all nations: a light for revelation to the Gentiles, and the glory of your people Israel" (verses 29–32).

In other words, "Lord, I am ready to die now. I've seen the Promised One."

Simeon finished well.

Anna, an old woman who never left the Temple day and night, worshiping, fasting, praying, knew the moment she saw Jesus that He was the Promised Messiah. She erupted into praise, giving "thanks to God and spoke about the child to all who were looking forward to the redemption of Jerusalem" (Luke 2:38).

Anna finished well.

Caleb is one of my heroes. He not only stood against the tidal wave of unbelief when reporting back to Moses as one of the twelve men sent to explore the land of Israel's inheritance, but he seemed to have maintained that attitude of faith throughout his life. As an 85-year-old man he marched up to Joshua and boldly yet humbly declared,

> "Here I am today, eighty-five years old! I am still as strong today as the day Moses sent me out; I'm just as vigorous to go out to battle now as I was then. Now give me this hill country that the LORD promised me that day. You yourself heard then that the Anakites were there and their cities were large and fortified, but, the LORD helping me, I will drive them out just as he said."
>
> Joshua 14:10–12

Caleb's words amuse me. I think he may have been stretching things just a bit. I seriously doubt that he was as physically vigorous and strong as he was forty years earlier, but he was still strong in heart and soul—in spite of the fact that he had lived among a nation of unbelievers for forty years.

Another thing amuses me. Caleb knew he needed younger men to help him, and he knew how to recruit them: "I will give my daughter Aksah in marriage to the man who attacks and captures Kiriath Sepher [a neighboring town of Hebron]" (Joshua 15:16).

In other words, "Yes, I told Joshua I am still strong, but I do realize that I need help from younger men."

Othniel picked up the challenge, won the battle, married Caleb's daughter, then became the first judge of the nation of Israel.

Caleb finished well.

David had his share of failures, serious failures—adultery, murder—sins that brought devastation to his family and to the nation. But his heart kept turning back to the Lord. The psalms are filled with his heart-wrenching sobs of repentance as well as his exultant praise. Centuries later God seemed to have completely forgotten all of David's past sins when He described Israel's king as "a man after my own heart; he will do everything I want him to do" (Acts 13:22).

I like that! That Scripture fills me with joy. God forgets our past if we keep pressing in for more of Him. I, too, am "a man after God's heart." I may not yet fully have His heart, but I am "after" His heart.

David finished well.

Two of the Lord's chosen apostles also challenge me. One of them is the aged John, exiled on the island of Patmos because of his faith. We never hear one moment of complaint. He is so surrendered to the Lord in his old age that the Lord entrusts him with visitations and visions that have inspired and challenged believers through all the centuries. This saint of God was not impressed with his own importance. He was simply "your brother and companion in the suffering" (Revelation 1:9). What glory must have surrounded him in those closing days of his life! Suffering? Yes, but the glory of Jesus shone through him.

John finished well.

Who can ever forget Paul's words from the Roman jail: "For to me, to live is Christ and to die is gain" (Philippians 1:21). "I have learned the secret of being content in any and every situation, whether well fed or hungry, whether living in plenty or in want. I can do all this through him who gives me strength" (Philippians 4:12–13).

Or those inimitable last words to Timothy:

> The time for my departure is near. I have fought the good fight, I have finished the race, I have kept the faith. Now there is in store for me the crown of righteousness, which the Lord, the righteous Judge, will award to me on that day—and not only to me, but also to all who have longed for his appearing.
>
> 2 Timothy 4:6–8

Paul finished strong. History tells us that he was martyred for his faith.

I want to finish well. I want to be a Paul, a John, a Simeon, an Anna, a Caleb, a David. I want to go out in a blaze of glory, whether as a free man or a martyr, whether preaching from a pulpit or, like Stephen, under a volley of stones. When it is my time to go, I want to be able to look into the face of Jesus and say, "Thank You, Lord. You have led me and refined me and protected me and allowed me to participate with You in Your purpose for these last days. I have finished what You called me to do. I am ready to go."

Appendix A

Finto Bible Reading Plan

I have tried all kinds of Bible reading plans. You probably have, too.

I tried the plan that requires you to carry a reading outline folded in your Bible and check off each chapter as you read. I always lost the paper before the year was up.

Three chapters a day and five on Sunday took me through the Bible in a year, but I was not wanting to spend the majority of my time solely in the Old Covenant writing—and which of us can be sure we will read that many chapters daily?

I finally came up with a plan of my own that has worked for me for years. All I need is my reading Bible and a pencil.

I read from five different sections of Scripture: (1) the historical section of Genesis through Esther; (2) the poetry books of Job through Song of Solomon; (3) the prophets Isaiah through Malachi; (4) the Gospels and Acts; and (5) Romans through Revelation.

If I was beginning today and was reading from each section, I would read Genesis 1, Job 1, Isaiah 1, Matthew 1, and Romans 1, putting a small number for the year in which I am reading (8 for 2018, 9 for 2019, 0 for 2020 and so on) at the end of each chapter so that I know where I left off in that section even if I do not return there for several days.

Why has this been a good plan for me? Because I stay in all sections of Scripture at all times, and I am never behind or ahead. If I only read one chapter today because I am consumed with the message, or I simply do not take the time to read that day, I am not behind. If I should read all 66 chapters of Isaiah in one sitting, I am not ahead. Never behind. Never ahead. Just reading and meditating.

So if you are not sure you have read through the whole Bible, try my plan. If you have tried all kinds of plans and failed, try mine. If you do not like staying in the Old Testament so much of the time, but want to be sure you are reading also from the New Testament daily or almost daily, try this plan. I continue to be amazed at the fresh revelation that comes from Scripture.

Appendix B

Translations
of the Greek *Thlipsis*

Joseph Henry Thayer's *Greek-English Lexicon of the New Testament* (Baker, 1984) gives the definition of the Greek word θλιψις (*thlipsis*) as "pressing, pressing together, pressure, oppression, affliction, tribulation, distress, straits."

Fifteen times, *thlipsis* is translated "trouble(s)":

Mark 4:17; Matthew 13:21: "When trouble . . . comes"

John 16:33: "In this world you will have trouble"

Acts 7:10: "rescued him from all his troubles"

Romans 2:9: "trouble and distress for every human being who does evil"

Romans 8:35: "trouble or hardship or persecution"

1 Corinthians 7:28: "Those who marry will face many troubles"

2 Corinthians 1:4: "comforts us in all our troubles"

2 Corinthians 1:8: "the troubles we experienced"

2 Corinthians 4:17: "our light and momentary troubles"

2 Corinthians 6:4: "As servants of God, we commend ourselves . . . in troubles"

2 Corinthians 7:4: "In all our troubles my joy knows no bounds"

Philippians 1:17: "supposing that they can stir up trouble for me"

Philippians 4:14: "It was good of you to share in my troubles"

2 Thessalonians 1:6: "[God] will pay back trouble to those who trouble you"

Seven times, the word is translated "distress":

Matthew 24:21: "There will be great distress, unequaled"

Mark 13:19: "Those will be days of distress unequaled"

Matthew 24:29: "immediately after the distress of those days"

Mark 13:24: "in those days, following that distress"

2 Corinthians 2:4: "I wrote you out of great distress"

1 Thessalonians 3:7: "In all our distress and persecution we were encouraged"

James 1:27: "Look after orphans and widows in their distress"

Seven times, the word is translated "suffering(s)":

Acts 7:11: "Famine struck all Egypt . . . bringing great suffering"

Romans 5:3: "We also glory in our sufferings"

Romans 5:3: "Suffering produces perseverance"

Ephesians 3:13: "not to be discouraged because of my sufferings"

1 Thessalonians 1:6: "in the midst of severe suffering"

Revelation 1:9: "companion in the suffering"

Revelation 2:22: "will cast [Jezebel] on a bed of suffering"

Two times, the word is translated "hardships":

Acts 14:22: "through many hardships to enter the kingdom of God"

Acts 20:23: "The Holy Spirit warns me that prison and hardships are facing me"

Two times, the word is translated "trial(s)":

2 Corinthians 8:2: "in the midst of a very severe trial"

1 Thessalonians 3:3: "that no one would be unsettled by these trials"

Three times, the word is translated "affliction(s)":

Romans 12:12: "patient in affliction"

Colossians 1:24: "what is still lacking in regard to Christ's afflictions"

Revelation 2:9: "I know your afflictions"

Four times, the word is translated "persecution(s)":

Acts 11:19: "scattered by the persecution"

2 Thessalonians 1:4: "your perseverance . . . in all the persecutions"

Hebrews 10:33: "You were publicly exposed to insult and persecution"

Revelation 2:10: "You will suffer persecution for ten days"

Once, the word is translated "tribulation":

Revelation 7:14: "they who have come out of the great tribulation"

Once, the word is translated "anguish":

John 16:21: "When her baby is born she forgets the anguish"

Once, the word is translated "hard pressed":

2 Corinthians 8:13: "while you are hard pressed"

Appendix C

Translations of the Greek
Thumos and *Orge*

Two Greek words are translated "wrath" in our Bibles: *thumos* (θυμος) and *orge* (οργη). The King James Version translates *thumos* as "wrath" fifteen times; "fierceness," twice; and "indignation," once. *Orge* is translated "wrath" 31 times; "anger," three times; "indignation," once; and "vengeance," once. The following shows the translations in the New International Version. The important thing is that believers are protected from the wrath of God.

> Matthew 3:7; Luke 3:7: "Who warned you to flee from the coming wrath [*orge*]?"
> Mark 3:5: "[Jesus] looked around at them in anger [*orge*]."
> Luke 4:28: "All the people in the synagogue were furious [*thumos*] when they heard this."

Luke 21:23: "[Jesus predicted] great distress in the land and wrath [*orge*] against this people."

John 3:36: "Whoever rejects the Son . . . God's wrath [*orge*] remains on [him]."

Acts 19:28: "When [Paul's hearers] heard this, they were furious [*thumos*] and began shouting."

Romans 1:18: "The wrath [*orge*] of God is being revealed from heaven."

Romans 2:5: "[The disobedient are] storing up wrath [*orge*] against yourself for the day of God's wrath [*thumos*]."

Romans 2:8: "For those who . . . reject the truth . . . there will be wrath [*orge*] and anger [*thumos*]."

Romans 3:5: "If our unrighteousness brings out God's righteousness more clearly, what shall we say? That God is unjust in bringing his wrath [*orge*]?"

Romans 4:15: "The law brings wrath [*orge*]."

Romans 5:9: "[Believers are] saved from God's wrath [*orge*]."

Romans 13:4: "[The governing authorities] are God's servants, agents of wrath [*orge*]."

Romans 13:5: "It is necessary to submit to the authorities, not only because of possible punishment [*orge*]. . . ."

2 Corinthians 12:20: "[Paul feared that he would find] discord, jealousy, fits of rage"[*thumos*]."

Galatians 5:19–20: "Acts of the flesh [include] fits of rage [*thumos*]."

Ephesians 2:3: "We were by nature deserving of wrath [*orge*]."

Ephesians 4:31: "Get rid of all bitterness, rage [*thumos*] and anger [*orge*]."

Ephesians 5:6: "Because of such things God's wrath [*orge*] comes on those who are disobedient."

Colossians 3:6: "Because of these, the wrath [*orge*] of God is coming."

Colossians 3:8: "Rid yourselves of all such things as these: anger [*orge*], rage [*thumos*]."

1 Thessalonians 1:10: "Jesus . . . rescues us from the coming wrath [*orge*]"

1 Thessalonians 2:16: "The wrath [*orge*] of God has come upon them at last."

1 Thessalonians 5:9: "God did not appoint us to suffer wrath [*orge*]."

1 Timothy 2:8: "I want the men everywhere to [lift] up holy hands without anger [*orge*]."

Hebrews 3:11; 4:3: "I declared on oath in my anger [*orge*]. . . ."

Hebrews 11:27: "By faith [Moses] left Egypt, not fearing the king's anger [*thumos*]."

James 1:19: "Be . . . slow to become angry [*orge*]."

James 1:20: "Human anger [*orge*] does not produce the righteousness that God desires."

Revelation 6:16: "Hide us from the face of him who sits on the throne and from the wrath [*orge*] of the Lamb!"

Revelation 6:17: "The great day of [God's] wrath [*orge*] has come."

Revelation 11:18: "The nations were angry, and your wrath [*orge*] has come."

Revelation 12:12: "[The devil] is filled with fury [*thumos*]."

Revelation 14:8: "'Fallen is Babylon the Great,' which made all the nations drink the maddening [*thumos*] wine of her adulteries."

Revelation 14:10: "They . . . will drink the wine of God's fury [*thumos*] . . . [from the] cup of his wrath [*orge*]."

Notes

Chapter 2: Listen to the Right Report

1. Much more is recorded about this amazing revival in Brother Yun and Paul Hattaway's book, *The Heavenly Man: The Remarkable True Story of Chinese Christian Brother Yun* (Grand Rapids: Kregel, 2002).

2. For more information see https://www.irisglobal.org/about/history.

3. Bilquis Sheikh and Richard H. Schneider, *I Dared to Call Him Father: The Miraculous Story of a Muslim Woman's Encounter with God* (Minneapolis: Chosen, 2003).

Chapter 3: Expect the Harvests

1. Daniel James Levine and Sophia Lee, "Fleeing Hell," *World*, March 22, 2014.

2. Paul Joseph Watson, "Western-Backed 'Arab Spring' Leads to Persecution of Christians," Prison Planet.com, March 27, 2013, https://www.prisonplanet.com/western-backed-arab-spring-leads-to-persecution-of-christians.html.

3. This, according to personal report from a conversation with some of China's key leaders in the movement.

4. Brother Danyun, *Lilies Amongst Thorns* (Kent, England: Sovereign World, Ltd., 1991).

5. See, for instance, Daniel Wiser, "China Ramping Up Persecution of Christians," *Washington Free Beacon*, July 29, 2014.

6. Krikor Markarian, "Today's Iranian Revolution: How the Mullahs Are Leading the Nation to Jesus," *Mission Frontiers*, September 1, 2008.

7. Tass Saada, *Once an Arafat Man* (Carol Stream, Ill.: Tyndale House, 2008), Kindle edition.

8. Ibid.

9. Ibid.

Chapter 5: Pay Attention to God's Calendar

1. By the time of the King James translation in AD 1611, the celebration of Easter for the resurrection was deeply entrenched in Church culture, a culture dating back at least to the times of Emperor Constantine and the Nicene Council, when Constantine requested that the bishops find another day to celebrate the resurrection, rather than the date on which the Jewish people observed Passover.

2. Aviv is not the only one of God's calendar months mentioned by name in Scripture. Ten of the twelve months are named, though not all the names are still in use on the typical Hebrew calendar. Ziv, also called Iyar, is the second month (see 1 Kings 6:1, 37). Sivan is month three (see Esther 8:9). Months four and five, Tammuz and Av, have no biblical reference, but the sixth month is Elul (see Nehemiah 6:15); the seventh month is Ethanim, also called Tishrei (see 1 Kings 8:2); the eighth month is Bul, also called Cheshvan (see 1 Kings 6:38); the ninth month is Kislev (see Nehemiah 1:1–2; Zechariah 7:1); the tenth month is Tebeth, also called Tevet (see Esther 2:16); the eleventh month is Shebut, also called Sh'vat (see Zechariah 1:7); and the twelfth month is Adar (see Ezra 6:15; Esther 3:7, 13; 8:1; 9:1–21). These have all found their way into the biblical narrative.

Chapter 6: Glory in Suffering

1. David Pawson, *When Jesus Returns* (London: Hodder & Stoughton Publishers, 2003), 199.

2. See Appendix B: Translations of the Greek *Thlipsis*.

3. Richard Wurmbrand. *Tortured for Christ* (Bartlesville, Okla.: Living Sacrifice Book Company, 1993. Originally published by The Voice of the Martyrs, Inc., formerly called Christian Missions to the Communist World, Inc., 1967), 36.

4. Ibid., 45.

5. Ibid., 101.

Chapter 7: Escape God's Wrath

1. I will be discussing my own view of the Rapture in the next chapter.

2. See Appendix C: Translations of the Greek *Thumos* and *Orge*.

Chapter 8: Watch for the Signs

1. Iain H. Murray, *The Puritan Hope: Revival and the Interpretation of Prophecy* (Carlisle, Pa.: The Banner of Truth Trust, 1971, reprinted 1998), 72. This book is the source of this and other quotations from such notable men of faith as Jonathan Edwards and Charles Spurgeon.

2. Ibid., 46.

3. Ibid., 114.

4. Ibid., 256.

5. Richard Ostling, "The Jesus Revolution," *Time*, June 21, 1971, 39, 62.

6. Drew Desilver, "Jewish essentials: For most American Jews, ancestry and culture matter more than religion," *Pew Research Center*, October 1, 2013, http://www.pewresearch.org/fact-tank/2013/10/01/jewish-essentials-for-most-american-jews-ancestry-and-culture-matter-more-than-religion/.

7. For more information see: www.ad2000.org.

8. For more information see: https://table71.org/about/.

9. For more information see: https://joshuaproject.net/about/details.

10. For more information see: https://www.call2all.org/about/.

11. "2013 at the UN: 21 resolutions against Israel, 4 on rest of the world," *UN Watch* (blog), November 25, 2013, http://blog.unwatch.org/index.php/2013/11/25/this-years-22-unga-resolutions-against-israel-4-on-rest-of-world/.

Chapter 9: Do Not Be Deceived

1. Jim Walker, compiler, "The Christianity of Hitler revealed in his speeches and proclamations," February 27, 1997, additions June 3, 2006, http://nobelief.com.

2. Eric Metaxas, *Bonhoeffer: Pastor, Martyr, Prophet, Spy* (Nashville: Thomas Nelson, 2010), 171, 174.

3. This is the summation of Martin Luther's 1543 published work, *On the Jews and Their Lies*, included in an article by Dr. Eric W. Gritsch, "Was Luther Anti-Semitic?," *Christianity Today* 39 (1993). Dr. Gritsch was the Maryland synod professor of Church history at Lutheran Theological Seminary in Gettysburg, Pennsylvania, and the director of the Institute for Luther Studies.

4. Metaxas, *Bonhoeffer*, 155.

5. Eric Metaxas, *Seven Men* (Nashville: Thomas Nelson, 2013), 102.

6. Richard Wurmbrand, *Tortured for Christ* (Bartlesville, Okla.: Living Sacrifice Book Company, 1998), 15. This book was first published by The Voice of the Martyrs formerly called Christian Mission to the Communist World, Inc., in 1967.

7. Ibid., 15–16.

8. Lee Strobel, *The Case for Christ* (Grand Rapids: Zondervan, 1998).

9. Keith DeRose, "Universalism and the Bible: The *Really* Good News," *Yale Campus Press*, winter 1998–99, https//campuspress.yale.edu/keith-derose-cv/.

10. John MacArthur, *Strange Fire: The Danger of Offending the Holy Spirit with Counterfeit Worship* (Nashville: Nelson Books, 2013), Kindle edition, introduction.

11. R. T. Kendall, *Holy Fire: A Balanced Biblical Look at the Holy Spirit's Work in Our Lives* (Lake Mary, Fla.: Charisma, 2014).

12. For more information see: http://www.startribune.com/elca-votes-to-allow-gay-pastors/53859967/.

13. For more information see: http://www.christianpost.com/article/20100709/pcusa-assembly-oks-removing-gay-ordination-ban/index.html.

14. Jonathan Merritt, "Eugene Peterson on changing his mind about same-sex issues and marriage," *On Faith and Culture, Religion News Service*, July 12, 2017, http://religionnews.com/2017/07/12/eugene-peterson-on-changing-his-mind-about-same-sex-issues-and-marriage/.

15. Jonathan Merritt, "Eugene Peterson backtracks on same-sex marriage," *On Faith and Culture, Religion News Service*, July 13, 2017, https://religionnews.com/2017/07/13/eugene-peterson-backtracks-on-same-sex-marriage/.

16. Rosaria Champagne Butterfield, *The Secret Thoughts of an Unlikely Convert: An English Professor's Journey into Christian Faith* (Pittsburg: Crown and Covenant Publications, 2012).

17. Dennis Jernigan, *Sing Over Me: An Autobiography* (Colliersville, Tenn.: Innova Publishing, 2014).

Chapter 11: Recapture Godly Imagination

1. Jim Rutz, "City Transformation on a Scale not Seen Before," *World Net Daily*, June 21, 2005, http://mobile.wnd.com/2005/06/30930/.

Chapter 12: Read the Book

1. Norman Williams and George Otis, *Terror at Tenerife* (Medford, Ore.: Omega Publications, 1977).

2. Hebrews 13:5 ESV.

3. Isaiah 43:1a.

4. Isaiah 43:1b.

5. Isaiah 43:2.

6. Adelle M. Banks, "The Bible—helpful, but not read much," *Religion News Service*, April 25, 2017, http://religionnews.com/2017/04/25/the-bible-helpful-but-not-read-much/.

Chapter 13: Pray the Word

1. James W. Goll, *Kneeling on the Promises* (Grand Rapids: Chosen, 1999).

Chapter 15: Call on Jesus

1. Shawn A. Akers, "Women Use Jesus' Name to Scare Away Robber," *Charisma*, March 2013, 20.

Chapter 17: Live in Community

1. Daniel Gruber, *Copernicus and the Jews*, vol. 1 of *The Separation of Church and Faith* (Hanover, N.H.: Elijah Publishing, 2005), 65.

2. Ibid. (and my own fluency in the German language).

3. Ibid., 66.

4. Ibid., 67.

5. Ibid., 65.

Chapter 19: Prophesy Life to Yourself

1. Go to our Caleb Company website at calebcompany.org to learn about the various training schools we offer, when students spend time in our Nashville, Tennessee, base, then a month in Israel.

Index

Shortly after **Don Finto** finished his undergraduate work at Abilene Christian (now) University and married Martha, they spent the next eight years in missions in post–World War II Germany, returning to the U.S. in 1960. After completion of additional post-graduate degrees from Harding University and Vanderbilt University, he joined the faculty at Lipscomb University in Nashville, Tennessee, teaching both German and Bible, and ultimately serving as head of the Modern Language Department.

In 1971 Don became the pastor of Belmont Church, serving as their senior leader for the next 25 years. He continues to serve as a pastor to pastors, and is widely known for his involvement with the resurrected community of Jewish believers in Jesus both in the United States and in Israel.

Don founded the Caleb Company in 1996, wanting to challenge people to emulate the biblical Caleb by (1) continuing to "take their mountains" even into old age, (2) raising up the next generations to be strong men and women of God and (3) remaining wholeheartedly devoted to God all the days of their lives.

Following Martha's homegoing in the spring of 2016, Don continues to be a father not only to his three children, seven grandchildren and nine great grandchildren, but also to a host of spiritual descendants and friends.

If you would like to connect with Don personally or find out more about the Caleb Company ministry, training schools, speaking engagements, trips to Israel or Jewish-related ministries, you may contact Don at www.calebcompany.org or in care of The Caleb Company, P.O. Box 493, Thompson Station, TN, 37179.

CALEB
COMPANY

EQUIPPING THE CHURCH
TO PARTICIPATE IN GOD'S
BIBLICAL PLAN FOR ISRAEL
AND ITS RELATIONSHIP TO
WORLD REVIVAL

WHAT DO WE DO?

OUR HISTORY

Caleb Company was started by Don Finto in 1996 as he was leaving the pastorate of Belmont Church in Nashville, TN. He named it Caleb Company because, like the biblical Caleb, Don wanted to raise up a company of warriors who would have "a different spirit" and who would follow the Lord "wholeheartedly" all their lives, who would raise up "descendants" who "will inherit the land," and to challenge old people to keep taking their mountains even into old age.

After serving in leadership with Youth With A Mission for fourteen years, Tod McDowell relocated his family to Nashville, Tennessee, in 2007 to work full-time with Caleb Company. In 2010, Tod became Executive Director. We have two beautiful properties in the country South of Nashville that host our ministry activities. We have an outstanding staff and yearly interns along with a constant flow of students.

WWW.CALEBCOMPANY.ORG

TRAINING & EQUIPPING:

Our training and ministry schools fulfill our mission of equipping the church to participate in God's Biblical plan for Israel and its relationship to world revival. We teach that intimacy with God is the fuel that enables us to walk in our God-given identity and destiny. We value intergenerational community that passionately embraces a lifestyle of worship and prayer, as we embrace God's heart for Israel and reach out to all nations.

SPEAKING & TEACHING:

We travel and speak extensively throughout the United States and across the world. Some of our consistent partnerships and ministry are with Youth With A Mission, Iris Global Ministry, International House of Prayer, Gateways Beyond, and Tikkun International. We teach on College campuses, missions and ministry schools as well as conferences and revival meetings.

CREATING RESOURCES:

We are called to create "weapons of mass instruction." Through inspiring books, in-depth curriculum, online training, teaching videos, blog posts, podcasts, and more. Our aim is to multiply the message of God's heart and purpose for Israel so all nations may understand and participate in God's Biblical plan for Israel and its relationship to world revival in our day.

More Dynamic Teaching from Don Finto!

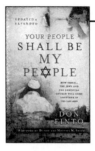